WIN YOUR CITY

Frank Purser

A Strategic Guide to Achieve and Sustain Revival in Your Community

Win Your City
A Strategic Guide to Achieve and Sustain Revival in Your Community
by Frank Purser

Printed in the United States of America

ISBN 9781619046078

www.xulonpress.com

Contents

Introduction

This book is about revival—citywide revival. If the systematic process described in this book is followed precisely, a majority of the population in your city will be saved, and those who are already Christian will become more fruitful. But before we can get to that, we must first ask the question, what is revival? What exactly does this word mean? There are differing views within the church as to what the word *revival* means, so let's take a closer look at it.

Revival comes from the root word *vivere*, which means "to live." Adding *re* in front changes the meaning to "to live again." So *to live again* means that whatever *was* living died, but it was resuscitated and came back to life. Many believe that this term *revival* refers to those in the church who have stepped away from their salvation and returned to living according to the values of the world; however, when they are revived, they return to their relationship with Jesus and the values of Christianity. Another interpretation of *revive* could just as easily refer to a second birth, the kind Jesus talks about in John 3:16. The person in this case has been born from his or her mother's womb and is then spiritually reborn, or "born again," as some like to term it.

Both meanings of revival are valid, and both are addressed in this book. Systematically, the unbelievers in a community cannot be born again without first having someone praying for them and the gospel shared with them. It is critical, therefore, that the body of believers within the community be revived to return to their Christian roots and receive a passion for those in the community who do not know Jesus. Both expressions of revival are needed for a citywide revival to take place.

Revival on a large scale is so close to God's heart that He has recently taken the initiative Himself to see it happen. God prefers to work through His children on earth but has sovereignly moved by His grace in cities like Brownsville, Florida; Toronto, Ontario; and Lakeland, Florida. Sometimes He even uses impure vessels. Nevertheless, multitudes have entered the kingdom as a result of these sovereign moves of God.

I believe we need to get on board God's glory train and do the things necessary to make it easy for Him to work in our communities. We are engaged in a spiritual battle, and we need to render impotent the evil spiritual forces active in our communities. It is easy to do, but it does involve a concerted community effort.

How This Book Came About

A few years ago, I was going through an intense period of seeking God about what He wanted me to do. A ministry I was involved with had ended, so I was available and wanted to know what God had in mind for me next. The church I belonged to had a prayer chapel, a facility completely devoted to and anointed for prayer. I went there daily, both before work and after work, seeking and worshiping my Lord. I also fasted regularly, typically

Slowly, God began to unveil to me a plan, a process to win cities.

two days a week. This period of seeking God was intense and lasted for over a year.

During this time, God slowly began to unveil to me a plan, a process, to win cities for and with Him. The goal was to get the majority of a city born again and discipled. The process consisted of six major steps:

- Develop unity among the church leaders of the city.
- Develop unity and enthusiasm among the churches of the city.
- Pray for each and every person in the city over a protracted period of time, amplified by periodic citywide Concerts of Prayer.
- Blitz the community with abundant and relevant advertising.
- Hold evangelistic events continuously until the Holy Spirit said to stop.
- Disciple the new converts.

Once this strategy was developed in me, God began to develop each step within the strategy, giving scriptural basis for each step. This process took over a decade as the people and messages crossed my path and the Spirit of Wisdom and Revelation provided more clarity to the strategy.

The strategic principles described in this book will work anywhere, anytime, in any community, no matter its size or economic condition. These principles are biblical, and they will work if the believers in the community will only work them.

Many will look at the six steps and say that these are followed in any major evangelistic campaign. These steps were revealed to me independently of other campaign strategies. They did not come by researching past revivals or moves of God. Rather, they came by deeply soaking in God's presence and receiving from Him. Nevertheless, after subsequently studying other campaigns, I would agree, to a point

I have spoken to numerous evangelists who have shared that the degree of unity demonstrated in their campaigns—even though they desired and sought it—was often limited to having a few pastors sitting on the stage or in the front row. In most cases, preceding prayer by the community was very limited or nonexistent. No campaign has developed these steps to the level that is presented in this book, but the development of these steps to the degree described herein is absolutely crucial to achieve the desired result of citywide transformation. Once you read and study this revival guide in an attitude of prayer, I think you will agree.

You *can* win your city for Christ. Your city *can* return to Godly principles. And as each and every city in your state is won, your state will be revived. The effect will then snowball to a nation that once again reveres God.

The time is now. More and more frequently, pastors are gathering in unity to pray for their city. Churches have posted phone-book pages on their walls and prayed for the people they represent. It is happening: God is awakening the church to become the Bride of Christ, to bring in the harvest. This is the latter rain talked about by the prophet Joel. Let's walk in the rain together. Forget about the umbrellas—let's get soaked in God and bring about the person/community/state/nation transformation He most urgently desires. Let's respond to and follow His heartbeat.

Chapter 1

The Battle for Your Community

Deuteronomy 30 is about the choice of life or death. Death can reign in your city or Life can reign in your city. For a long time, our cities have experienced a gradual decay towards death, but we can change that. We can choose life and change that.

You have picked up this book because you have a desire to win your city for Christ. You sense the need to choose life. You realize that our society has digressed so much that only a move of God can fix it. But what are those community characteristics that have triggered you to action?

Perhaps school bullying has done it for you. This is an ever-increasing issue, and both school officials seem powerless to stop it. Even parents seem powerless to stop it. It seems to be stemming from a source so evil and powerful that it is like a raging flood in springtime. Seventy-seven percent of students are bullied mentally, verbally physically. One out of four students will be bullied this month. And at least half of all bullying incidents go unreported.

Bullying is increasingly viewed as an important contributor to youth violence, including homicide and suicide, and over 100,000 students carry a gun to school each day.

Fully 87 percent of students involved in shootings are motivated by a desire to get back at those who have hurt them. Each day 160,000 students miss school for fear of being bullied. Each month 282,000 students are physically attacked. Unfortunately, bullying isn't limited to only our schools. With the advent of sites like Facebook.com, cyber bullying is becoming more and more prominent. Bullying has to stop, and you can stop it in your community.

Or maybe the slaughter of the unborn is your pet peeve. Fully 1.6 million abortions are performed in the United States each year. That is approximately three every minute. Every minute three of God's precious creations die for the sake of convenience. Every four years we reach the number murdered in the Holocaust. What is the statistic in your community?

You can stop this terrible evil, and you don't have to parade in front of the clinic with a sign in your hand to do it. A citywide spiritual revolution is the key, and you can help make that happen. Imagine if the young pregnant lady who simply made a mistake was surrounded by those who loved her instead of those who condemned her. How would that change the situation? Countless Christian pregnancy centers have shown the power of love in action, and we need to make this our normal conduct. We don't need to change laws and stage protests at the clinics; we need to change the spiritual atmosphere.

Gambling was on the ballot for a number of years in my state. The gambling enterprises kept coming back every year even though they were defeated each year. Finally one year they won two initiatives. Their strategy of beating at the voter's door until the voter eventually tired and let them in finally worked.

Gambling in and of itself is not necessarily wrong. The stock market is a gamble, and essentially, all life is a gamble. But gambling in a dedicated business such as a casino can and does enslave people. Surely not every person who walks through the doors of such establishments is enslaved, just as not every person who enters a bar is an alcoholic. But there is a sinister force operating behind the scenes that preys on people's weaknesses. The evil voice whispers, "Just one more hand," "Just one more pull on the handle," or "Just one more push on the button." Before long, the person's will along with his money is lost, and he keeps trying to win that money back, only to dig an even deeper hole. This is especially insidious when in poor economic times, people turn to the casino in an attempt to win their daily bread. Sadly, they often make their situation much worse and may develop an addiction in the process. Gambling is a symptom of a morally weak society. But we can change that. *You* can change that.

Love, true biblical love, the kind that accepts you just the way you are and loves you just the way you are, with no preconceived expectations, is a foreign concept in today's society. This kind of love can come only from Jesus as we allow Him to love through us. There is a hole inside each of us that craves this kind of love and acceptance. When we don't find it, we search for it in areas the devil provides: gangs, motorcycle clubs, pimps and prostitution, anything to even partially fill that void.

Gangs have been on the rise over the last few decades and, combined with violent motorcycle clubs, are the largest drug-distribution network in America. They are also the largest source of violent crime. But it all stems from the hole inside each of us. If we understand this root cause, we can reverse the effect. We can break the curse over gang members' lives and show them the only person who can fill that hole. We have Jesus, and He can fix this. We can stop the gang problem in our cities.

These are just a few examples or symptoms of the decay in our society—in your own community. But you can see it everywhere. The workplace is becoming more and more devoid of love and caring for coworkers and employees. Consider also driving. Courtesy used to be the rule, and allowing someone to merge in front of you used to be standard behavior. Now it is a rare occurrence. Selfishness seems to be the order of the day, and the problem is, it is a virus that even works its way into the way *we* respond and act.

But how did our society and your community in particular arrive at this state? In 1 Peter 5:8, the Bible says that the devil roams around seeking whom he may devour. And that is exactly what he has done. He has roamed through our schools (we gave away praying there a long time ago). He has found opportunity in the evil desires of our kids' hearts. Lack of love in our churches and families and among those in our communities has resulted in kids and even adults attempting to find love and acceptance somewhere. Gangs and cruelty have resulted. We, through our lack of love, have created the opportunity for the devil to come in unhindered. It is our fault, and we need to repent.

But there is an antidote. There is a solution to this decay, and His name is Jesus. We *can* restore our communities; *you* can restore *your* community. But it will require action. You cannot sit back in your easy chair, watching television, and expect this to turn around. You have to do something. Are you willing to do something? Are you willing to do what is necessary to win back your city?

Are you willing to do something? Are you willing to do what is necessary to win back your city?

You may ask, "What can I do? I am just one person." Of course you are. But do you have a private daily prayer time? In most cases, when a community has deteriorated, it is because the people of God have stopped praying. They have stopped declaring that Jesus is Lord over their city. However, God says in 2 Chronicles 2:14 that if we, those who are called by His name, humble ourselves and cry out to Him and turn from our wickedness, then He will heal our land. Can you fall on your face before God? Can you turn from your wickedness, your lack of love? Can you pay the price that is necessary? Can you reach out and receive the passion that Jesus has for the people of your community? Can you put love into action? There is a choice to be made, described in Deuteronomy 30. You can choose either life or death. Choose life today, and get on your knees!

A Spiritual Military Conquest Is Needed

Though Jesus soundly defeated the devil and made of him a public spectacle, the enemy is still present on this earth and remains very active. Jesus won back our communities for us, but they remain occupied by the enemy. Ephesians says we wrestle with rulers, authorities, powers, and spiritual forces of the dark world, not against flesh and blood.

The enemy works from an authority structure and has a leading demon in charge of each community. He also has several lieutenants to whom he has given authority in the various spheres of influence that he has gained over the years. He is the one goading the bully, influencing the gambler, guiding the drug pusher, controlling the alcoholic, and causing us not to pray. These areas of influence have only been seized as we, the body of Christ, have given him place. So it is really *our* fault. We have given our communities away.

Allowing the enemy to take control refers in part to the wicked ways talked about in 2 Chronicles. But the battle for your city is not over yet. You *can* take it back. It will, though, require a strategy and a concerted effort. The enemy is entrenched and will not easily give up the ground that he is occupying. He thinks of his rule as a military occupation, so we need to treat it the same. We need to conduct actual warfare using the weapons God has given us. So let's take a look at some military principles of war and align ourselves with them.

Throughout history, soldiers, military theorists, political leaders, philosophers, academic scholars, practitioners of international law, and human-rights advocacy groups have sought to determine fundamental rules for the conduct of warfare. One of the most famous and most often used documents detailing the truths of these fundamental rules is Sun Tzu's *Art of War*, written in the sixth century BC. Sun Tzu's writings are credited for the Viet Cong victory in the Vietnam War and provide the foundation for the principles of war developed by every major military command. This book is also still used by businesses worldwide to direct their business plans.

Sun Tzu listed only five factors, or principles, of war and developed them in thirteen chapters. Modern approaches have expanded and broken down those five principles differently, but the basic premise remains. The 2008 U.S. Army's *Field Manual FM-3-0*[1] lists the following basic principles of war:

- *Objective*: Direct every military operation toward a clearly defined, decisive, and attainable objective. The ultimate military purpose of war is the destruction of the enemy's armed forces and will to fight.
- *Offensive*: Seize, retain, and exploit the initiative. Even in defense, a military organization is expected to maintain a level of aggressiveness by patrolling and launching limited counteroffensives.
- *Mass*: Mass the effects of overwhelming combat power at the decisive place and time.
- *Economy of force*: Employ all combat power available in the most effective way possible; allocate minimum essential combat power to secondary efforts.

- *Maneuver*: Place the enemy in a position of disadvantage through the flexible application of combat power.
- *Unity of command*: For every objective, seek unity of command and unity of effort.
- *Security*: Never permit the enemy to acquire unexpected advantage.
- *Surprise*: Strike the enemy at a time or place or in a manner for which he is unprepared.
- *Simplicity*: Prepare clear, uncomplicated plans and concise orders to ensure thorough understanding.

These principles are not just mere ideas that generals have thought up. These are principles that time and again throughout history have proven to be true. They have decisively brought victory when wholly applied and, conversely, have brought defeat when ignored.

Our entrenched spiritual foe sees his stance as a military occupation that he has gained through legal means that we have allowed. He is, however, only loosely organized and operates through deception, using guerrilla warfare. As we consider each of the principles of war, it becomes easy to see how the enemy has insidiously used each one when we were not looking. So let us look at these principles more closely, align them with the principles in the Bible, and see how they can be used in a strategic campaign to win back our cities.

> *Objective*: Direct every military operation toward a clearly defined, decisive, and attainable objective. "The ultimate military purpose of war is the destruction of the enemy's armed forces and will to fight."

As Stephen Covey once said, we must "begin with the end in mind." To do so, we must develop a very clear overall objective and from that objective develop our strategy. If there is no objective, if we just whittle away at the enemy piece by piece without an overall objective, then the war will simply not be won. The leaders of the church in the city must strategize and develop an overall objective for winning their city.

As Sun Tzu would say, "We must know our enemy." We must understand that the enemy is not the bar owner, the bully, or the doctor in the abortion clinic. Paul defines our enemy in Ephesians 6:12 this way: "For our struggle is not against flesh and blood, but against the rulers, against the authorities, against the powers of this dark world and against the spiritual forces of evil in the heavenly realms."

Jesus gives us our objective against this enemy in three places:

> Then Jesus came to them and said, "All authority in heaven and on earth has been given to me. Therefore *go and make disciples* of all nations, baptizing them in the name of the Father and of the Son and of the Holy Spirit, and teaching them to obey everything I have commanded you. And surely I am with you always, to the very end of the age."
> —MATTHEW 28:18–20, EMPHASIS ADDED

> He said to them, "Go into all the world and preach the gospel to all creation. Whoever believes and is baptized will be saved, but whoever does not believe will be condemned. And these signs will accompany those who believe: In my name they will drive out demons; they will speak in new tongues; they will pick up snakes with their hands; and when they drink deadly poison, it will not hurt them at all; they will place their hands on sick people, and they will get well."
> —MARK 16:15–18

> But you will receive power when the Holy Spirit comes on you; and you will be my witnesses in Jerusalem, and in all Judea and Samaria, and to the ends of the earth.
> —ACTS 1:8

Our objective is to win the lost of the city and then disciple them. As they are discipled and taught to give no place to the devil, then the devil will no longer be entrenched and will have no authority in the city. This requires a declaration of war, and the church leadership in the city must develop and declare the clear objective to take back the city. A couple of secular examples that highlight this point are as follows:

> No matter how long it may take us to overcome this premeditated invasion, the American people, in their righteous might, will win through to *absolute victory*. . . . With confidence in our armed forces, with the unbounding determination of our people, we will gain the *inevitable triumph*. So help us God.
> —President Franklin D. Roosevelt
> December 8, 1941
> emphasis added

> After all that has just passed, all the lives taken and all the possibilities and hopes that died with them, it is natural to wonder if America's future is one of fear. Some speak of an age of terror. I know there are struggles ahead and dangers to face. But this country will define our times, not be defined by them. As long as the United States of America is determined and strong, this will not be an age of terror; this will be an age of liberty, here and across the world.
>
> Great harm has been done to us. We have suffered great loss. And in our grief and anger, we have found our mission and our moment. Freedom and fear are at war. The advance of human freedom, the great achievement of our time and the great hope of every time, now depends on us. *Our nation—this generation—will lift a dark threat of violence from our people and our future*. We will rally the world to this cause by our efforts, by our courage. *We will not tire; we will not falter; and we will not fail*.

PRESIDENT GEORGE W. BUSH
SEPTEMBER 20, 2001
EMPHASIS ADDED

Offensive: Seize, retain, and exploit the initiative. Even in defense, a military organization is expected to maintain a level of aggressiveness by patrolling and launching limited counteroffensives.

We must use scriptural principles to seize, retain, and exploit the initiative. In chapter 2 of this book, we will discuss and apply the principle of unity found in Psalm 133. This principle renders the enemy powerless. However, even though he is powerless, he will continue to fight. In some cities, unity has been attained, yet the initiative has not been seized. The people go about their lives, enjoying their newly discovered unity and love towards one another. That may be fine and good, but there is a promise associated with this psalm that must be seized, retained, and exploited to completely rout the enemy. The promise must be implemented by faith. Carpe diem—seize the day. Seize the opportunity! Seize the promise! The advantage is now ours. God has rendered the enemy powerless; it is up to us to walk in it and seize and enjoy the victory.

Note that this principle of war carries forward to peacetime following the victory. This initiative gained through the principle of Psalm 133 must be maintained even after the victory is won. The enemy is not going to give up easily, and even though expelled from the city, he will attempt to return at every opportunity. We must maintain a level of aggressiveness against him, oppose him at every attempt, and give no place to him.

Mass: Mass the effects of overwhelming combat power at the decisive place and time.

The principle of overwhelming force implies, for your battle, the entire church in your city. But it is not just the church in your city, for there are those outside your city who would come alongside in prayer to participate in this battle of the kingdom. The Bible says one can put one thousand to flight, but two can put ten thousand to flight. Apply this multiplication principle to uniting the entire church in your city and the effect is staggering.

Have you ever read Frank Peretti's book *This Present Darkness*? Mr. Peretti portrays a spiritual battle for a city and shows the spiritual side of it with angels and demons in warfare. The Christians' role in this warfare consisted of alignment with the side of light as well as prayer and praise. The alignment with light brought more angelic forces into the fray, while the prayer and praise gave the angels their strength. Conversely, the alignment with darkness gave the demons their numbers and strength. I believe that God gave Mr. Peretti significant revelation about the workings of the spiritual realm as he conceived and wrote this novel. Imagine the impact of united prayer and praise on the forces of darkness in your community. It is truly an *overwhelming force*.

Only by winning the lost and discipling them can believers attain true transformation and victory in their city.

Consider the story of Elisha and his servant in 2 Kings 6:15–17. Elisha's servant was really fretting about how big a force was arrayed against Israel. Elisha simply said that their side was bigger and asked God to open his servant's eyes. The servant looked again and saw a massive angelic army that far exceeded the opposing demonic army. We need to understand that God is supporting our actions in the heavenlies with a massive angelic army that is double the size of Satan's. (Satan left heaven with only a third of the angelic host.) However, we must do what is required of us to both increase the angelic army and to empower it. United action by the church in the city creates an overwhelming force in the unseen heavenlies above the city.

The focal point for this overwhelming force is the lost in the city. Only by winning the lost and discipling them can believers attain true transformation and victory in their city. Once the majority of the people in the city become new believers, the devil has lost all influence. He is effectively kicked out of your city.

> *Economy of Force*: Employ all combat power available in the most effective way possible; allocate minimum essential combat power to secondary efforts.

During this battle to win back your city, other initiatives of the church must take a backseat. Essentially all of the church's effort should be focused on this battle. Imagine a general in a war who was also trying to run his business back home. The impact on the war would be disastrous. The church must have, for a period of time, absolute singleness of purpose. Yes, normal life activities must continue, with normal prayer times, normal worship, normal prayer for the sick. But all the church activities should refocus on the battle at hand.

> *Maneuver*: Place the enemy in a position of disadvantage through the flexible application of combat power.

This entire battle is a surprise to the enemy. He really is not all that smart—cunning maybe, but not smart. He was ecstatic when Jesus was hung on the cross, but he was totally taken by surprise when a few hours later Jesus showed up on his doorstep and whipped him up one side and down the other and then made a public spectacle of him. He could not figure out the simple passages of Scripture that brought Jesus to the cross, nor could he comprehend Genesis 3:15. He is stupid; he is lazy. He cannot create; he can only steal. He is quite happy with the complacency of the city church, and he is basically caught napping when the church arises.

The combat power here is simply love, prayer, unity, and the Word of God. Once the church begins to use the Word of God and pray in unison, the enemy is caught completely off guard and cannot produce an adequate defense. As you will see later, you must stop all negative skirmishes with the devil, and instead focus on love. The devil has no defense for this.

> *Unity of Command*: For every objective, seek unity of command and unity of effort.

In my mind, this principle must come first, not sixth. How can you develop an objective and corresponding strategy without the unity of the church leadership? But then, the principles of war were developed by military professionals where chain of command is an absolute, something practiced every minute of every day. So the principle of unity of command is rather obvious in military circles. The church, however, has not been operating as a military organization, so unity of command is a much more foreign concept to them. It therefore needs to be emphasized first in order to win back the city. This principle and the scriptural basis for it are developed in detail in both chapters 2 and 3 of this book.

Essentially, the church leadership throughout the city must unite. They must become one under a banner of love. This unity carries with it a promise of revival that God will fulfill as the leaders walk in it. Then they must develop their objective, their declaration of war, and establish the organizational structure of the offensive and the strategy to attain the objective. The church as a whole must then come together under the same banner of love, and together they will bring down the strongholds erected throughout the city.

> *Security*: Never permit the enemy to acquire unexpected advantage.

There is no way that we can keep the enemy from hearing our plans. However, remember that there are also demons named chaos, despair, and confusion (James 3:16). As long as we maintain the offensive—something the enemy is totally unprepared for—the foe will be disorganized and unable to mount a proper counteroffensive, much less acquire an unexpected advantage.

There are tactics that the enemy may use, however, to minimize the effect of our offensive and to try to gain an advantage. Two primary ones are strife and sin. (Both were used by the enemy in Peretti's novel.) The Bible exhorts us to make every effort to maintain the bond of peace (Eph. 4:3). Of course, we also need to maintain ourselves pure and we need to especially pray for our church leaders in this regard.

One of the most impressive moves of God's grace in the past few years was the move of God in Lakeland, Florida. Thousands upon thousands were saved and healed in this great outpouring, but do we or those in the world remember it this way? No. This was an extraordinary move of God, producing marvelous results, but what is remembered is the blemish that the devil put on it as it was concluding. I do not lay the blame on the individuals involved. The blame belongs on the doorstep of the church. *Someone wasn't praying!* As a result, the enemy acquired an unexpected advantage.

We must be extra careful not to let this happen and to take extra steps to ensure that it does not. We must not let the enemy acquire unexpected advantage. Remember, the leadership of the strategic offensive is where the devil will apply the principle of economy of force. Just expect this, and keep a giant hedge of prayer protection around your leaders.

> *Surprise*: Strike the enemy at a time or place or in a manner for which he is unprepared.

The enemy is totally unprepared for our offensive against him. He has been very happy with the complacency of the church (much to our discredit) and has grown fat in his laziness. When we launch an offensive against him, he is totally surprised and totally unprepared.

> *Simplicity*: Prepare clear, uncomplicated plans and concise orders to ensure thorough understanding.

This is an obvious but much overlooked principle. However, the leadership of the church in your city is very good at implementing this principle. They are used to taking Scripture and making it simple and understandable each and every week from the pulpit. This same effort needs to take place as the strategy is developed to win back your city.

So you see, it is possible and even simple (though not necessarily easy) to win back your city. Fully applying these principles of warfare guarantees success each and every time. All you have to do is apply them and walk in them. And this book shows you how.

The art of war owns certain elements and fixed principles. We must acquire that theory, and lodge it in our heads—otherwise, we will never get very far. FREDERICK THE GREAT

[1] The Army Field Manual is a non-copyrighted publication approved for public release with an unlimited distribution. It is available free of charge in PDF format from various sources on the internet.

Chapter 2

Unity: The Driving Force

You have picked up this book because you have a desire to win your city for Christ. Perhaps you asked God how to do it and then this book was brought to your attention. Well, the first step is truly going to be the hardest—unity. Without unity, every step is like climbing a sand dune: three steps forward and two back. With unity, every step becomes smooth, straight, and level.

This is a battle. The devil has a stronghold over nearly every single community. And he is not going to let go easily. God, however, has provided a way to render him and his cohorts impotent. It's in Psalm 133:

> How good and pleasant it is when brothers dwell together in unity. . . for there the Lord commanded His blessing, even life forevermore.

When God commands something, the devil just does not have a chance. God's command has to come to pass. But what is the Lord commanding here in Psalm 133? The blessing stated is "life forevermore," or everlasting life. Everlasting life can be achieved only through the redemptive work of Jesus. Everlasting death, or everlasting torment, is the only other option. We all are intimately aware of these two options.

Psalm 133 essentially says that unity brings revival. But not only does it bring revival, but God *commands* the revival. Does this mean that once we dwell in unity people are just going to flock into church to get saved? Perhaps and, to a degree, yes. As with any promised blessing, there is a small amount of blessing that just naturally occurs, but God expects us to walk by faith so that the fruit of the blessing will be much more pronounced. As an example, in those rare places where the church has started to come together in unity, there is a marked increase in church attendance, even without a strategic initiative to reach the lost. But why is this, and just what has occurred in the heavenlies?

God's blessing and the unity blessing of revival tie the enemy's hands. He has no power to prevent the blessing—none, nada.

Consider Job. God was blessing this man big time. He loved God and was the richest guy around. He had blessing upon blessing. But he had one fear (Job 1:5), and this opened the door for the devil. But still, since Job had God's blessing, the devil had to ask permission to work havoc in his life. The devil's hands were tied unless God gave permission, and in this case, God was bound to give His permission because of Job's fear.

God's blessing and the unity blessing of revival tie the enemy's hands. He has no power to prevent the blessing—none, nada. The power to prevent salvation is broken! Acts 4:32–33 is a great example of this principle in action:

> All the believers were one in heart and mind. . . . With great power the apostles continued to testify to the resurrection of the Lord Jesus, and much grace was upon them all.

Unity yields a consequence. The apostles apparently knew this and walked in it with great power. Then strife and discord broke out regarding the distribution of food (food was also the first temptation of Jesus and the temptation of Adam). This strife and the corresponding disunity initiated a rapid downhill spiral. It resulted in the stoning of Stephen and increased persecution and dispersion of the church.

This dispersion may have been a good thing for the church, and from the persecution we ultimately got Paul (whatever the devil means for evil God turns around for good), but the unity and resulting power in the community were never again the same. It is not documented again that thousands were daily added to the church in Jerusalem as in the days when they first walked in unity. I think Peter learned a lesson from this also. Both of his letters, but especially the second one, have an overriding theme of maintaining harmony. Additionally, Paul says in Ephesians to make every effort to keep the unity of the Spirit through the bond of peace (Eph. 4:3).

Even without the promise of God's commanded blessing, unity has some distinct advantages in the battle for winning your city. Please remember that we *are* in a battle. Ephesians 6:12 says we wrestle not against flesh and blood, "but against the rulers, against the authorities, against the powers of this dark world and against the spiritual forces of evil in the heavenly realms." So we are in a battle, especially when we attempt to take back something that the enemy has claimed as his own.

Imagine a military force that is trying to defeat an entrenched enemy. This military force is made up of several different units that have captains who operate independently of each other. In fact, these captains do not even like each other and are jealous of each other's victories. They maybe even rejoice when another is defeated. When one captain is severely wounded, the other captains just sit back and watch and maybe talk about it among their troops, imagining how it happened and saying he probably deserved it or brought it on himself.

In such a scenario, one unit of this force might launch an offensive against part of the entrenched foe and maybe gain some ground, while another unit loses ground on another front. One captain might need some antiaircraft artillery, but alas, the unit on the other side of the city is in possession of that resource. The battle for the city is therefore never won, partly because each individual unit does not have all the weapons and specialties necessary for success, but mostly because there is no real unified strategic initiative.

Now consider the same units all united together under one banner and all supporting one another. Together they develop a strategic plan to defeat the entrenched foe. They plan to use the weapons and abilities of each unit where they are best served and even combine some of the units to make them stronger. They also plan to coordinate their attacks so that actual damage is done to the opposing entrenched force. The result is amazing! They now have the potential to actually defeat the enemy and take back the city. Unity of command and an overall objective that is systematically developed to produce subordinate objectives are very powerful principles.

Unfortunately, the condition in the city church today is even worse than the disorganized example described above. The church has *individuals* engaging in their own battles against the entrenched foe, even without the support of their church leaders. Maybe this happens because they don't know they need the support of leadership or because they don't want it; or maybe it happens because the leader does not want to give his support, for whatever reason. In these cases, personal, individual victories may be successful, but personal battles against an entrenched enemy by one or two individuals are generally doomed to failure.

Most churches do not have a strategic plan for winning the lost in their city, much less a plan shared with other churches. There are multitudes of people out there: businesspeople, engineers, technicians, professionals, college students, and children. People of all ages, economic statuses, and ethnic cultures are in a mad riotous race over a cliff to hell. Are we going to just sit back and watch them tumble over, or are we going to cry out to God and ask Him to give us a passion—the same passion He has—for the lost of our city?

There is a story in Genesis 11:4–6 about unity:

> Then they said, "Come, let us build ourselves a city, with a tower that reaches to the heavens, so that we may make a name for ourselves; otherwise we will be scattered over the face of the whole earth."
>
> But the LORD came down to see the city and the tower the people were building. The LORD said, "If as one people speaking the same language they have begun to do this, then nothing they plan to do will be impossible for them."

When brothers dwell together in unity, "nothing they plan to do will be impossible for them."

There are several keys to winning a city, but first and foremost is unity—unity first among the spiritual leaders of the city. This unity is paramount. If you truly want to win your city back you must put aside petty differences and *UNITE*. God really, really, really wants to win the lost in your city. This is His heartbeat. Sometimes He gets so impatient waiting for us to act that He just does it Himself. God wants to visit your city and win back all the lost. Of course, some won't respond to Him, because He has given them all free will, but if the concepts in this book are followed, MOST WILL. You just have to make it easy for them to come. And unity among church leaders is the key first step.

This is not to say that the individual parishes and denominations within the city do not continue to thrive. They are a beautiful display of God's diversity within the body. What is meant is that there is love between the various arms of the church, and each arm supports and works with the other, mutually building each other up. The gifts God gives to one arm are used by all the others.

> *There are a diversity of gifts and callings already resident within your city that are sufficient to wage a winning battle against your entrenched foe.*

The church today in any given city is made up of churches from many different denominations and organizations. A typical city may have Trinity Methodist, First Baptist, New Life Assembly of God, Grace Episcopal, Saint James Lutheran, Saint John Catholic, Crossroad Church of the Nazarene, and several other churches that don't fit these denominations. With very few exceptions, all these churches have a covering organization or hierarchy that probably provides oversight leadership from outside the community and most likely from outside the state. While this structure has the ability to mentor and provide doctrinal oversight for each church and its leaders, quite often it also produces division within the church in the city. Paul confronted this tendency head-on in Corinth and labeled it destructive (1 Corinthians 3:4–9).

The denominations set up by man are all valid expressions of the diversity found in the body of Christ. Nearly every one of them is based upon the teachings of a man that God raised up during his hour. That man, whether it was Charles Wesley, Martin Luther, or some other saint of God, had particular reasons for breaking from the establishment of that day to form a new worship style. However, some of these denominational dividing lines have remained in place even though the reasons for their emergence have long since dissipated.

God sees the church differently, though. Yes, He works within the structures we have set up, and He calls and appoints leaders within those structures. But within a given city, He sees only one church. Take a look at the second and third chapters of Revelation. Jesus is sending letters to the church in Ephesus, to the church in Smyrna, to the church in Pergamum, to the church in Thyatira, to the church in Philadelphia, and the list goes on. Paul wrote his letters to the churches in Corinth, Galatia, Thessalonica, Ephesus, Rome, and Colossae. As in New Testament times, God has established a church in your city that has a diversity of expressions. But God's intent is not for these expressions to be divisive—diverse, yes; divisive no. He fully expects each expression to walk in love, fully supporting the others. As Paul said to the church in Corinth, "For we are God's fellow workers."

In fact, somewhere in your city, God has provided everything that the church needs. For this citywide initiative, there will be a need for a skilled intercessor to lead and train other intercessors. That individual may be in one church while the bulk of the intercessors may be (and probably are) in others. One church may have a very skilled businessman who has the ability to raise the necessary funds, while another may have an excellent children's minister able to pull together an evangelistic children's campaign. There are a diversity of gifts and callings already resident within your city that are sufficient to wage a winning battle against your entrenched foe. God has not left your city defenseless. You *can* kick the devil out for good!

So there are three key things that unity produces in your city:

- Unity brings God's blessing of everlasting life; that is, revival, which strips the enemy of his power.
- Unity makes it possible to create a unified front in order to launch an effective strategic offensive.
- Unity brings about the critical union of gifts.

There is also a political ramification to unity. For at least the last century, the world has been watching the church and has seen a church fighting against itself. Divisions within the church and the church's inability to support itself have been the chief excuses for those outside the church not to come in. A show of unity within your community, however, smashes this excuse to smithereens. The early church so carried out the command of John 13:35 that pagans were forced to exclaim, "See how much they love one another!"

Achieving Unity Among the Church Leadership

You are probably beginning to recognize just how critical church unity is, but you may wonder how to get there. For decades the church has been operating denominationally, and denominations are okay. But primarily, the citywide church must become the emphasis. For far too long, it has been tolerated and even acceptable to criticize and dislike a fellow Christian pastor within the citywide church.

No more.

I said, *no more*.

Not if you want to change the spiritual atmosphere in your city.

This has to stop. The clergy of the city must display unity before the church ever will. So if you are a church leader—a pastor, priest, or leader by some other title—take an assessment of yourself as God sees you. How do you look at the pastor down the street? Do you think he is off his rocker because he speaks in tongues? Or maybe you just cannot get past that transmutation belief of that priest on the other side of town. Maybe you have actually said so in public or to your congregation. The point is, those other spiritual leaders are members of the body of Christ, and God has accepted that diversity. You need to also. God has called them to their positions of leadership, and that calling must be honored. The fact that you in your ignorance may not agree with them does not make their calling any less sure. God has accepted and called them—who do you think you are?

If you think you have the perfect church or perfect denomination, you are absolutely, positively mistaken. There is no such thing; it does not exist and never will—at least not in this age. However, God does call the church to become perfect (Eph. 4:13), but this is not talking about individual church bodies or denominations. It is talking about the entire church universal and more specifically the whole church in your community.

If you are a church leader, unity starts with you. You cannot pass the buck. God has called you to shepherd and lead, so you must lead and you must start. Start with any other leader you have a grudge with or against. Render an apology and ask for forgiveness. Ask God for forgiveness for this sin, because the failure to love your brother is just that—*sin*. Once this is done, begin to seek God about organizing an event to bring together the church leaders in your city. A breakfast in a neutral locality is probably best. Invite every single Christian church leader to attend so that each church is represented by its senior leader. Make it an offer they cannot refuse. Take authority over the enemy. Pray, pray, pray! God has to bring about this unity because the devil will certainly try to stop it from happening. In fact, he has sown these seeds of discord to keep you out of unity for a long, long time.

This breakfast should be held in a neutral place, bathed in prayer, and include the following elements:

- Breakfast
- Worship
- A message regarding the sin of church division
- Reconciliation

All followed by communion and a unity pledge signed by all.

Your speaker should come from within your citywide church body (the gift is already normally resident in your body), but certainly allow the Holy Spirit to direct you in this. Perhaps for your unique situation, someone from outside the city church would be more appropriate. Leave time before communion for individuals to make it right with others, if needed. Everyone should leave the meeting with a copy of this book in their hands because this book outlines the steps necessary to walk in the promise of God's commanded blessing.

If you are not a church leader, but God has nevertheless placed a heavy burden on your heart for unity and revival in your city, then your job initially is simply to pray. God often uses ordinary people like you and me to bring about an extraordinary miracle. And a miracle is indeed what is needed to effect unity. Establishing unity is *the* most difficult part of this strategy. But it is also the most important. Consider giving a copy of this book to your church leader, but do so in love and bathe it in much prayer. Begin to pray earnestly for your leader and for unity, and be prepared to do whatever God tells you to do to put feet to those prayers.

After Reconciliation

Do you remember when you were newly born again? It was such bliss, like coming out of a bad dream. You finally realized that there was a God and that He really loved you. You discovered a brand-new family too. However, you also gained a brand-new enemy. And he was just sitting out there watching and waiting for an opportunity to pull you back into his realm.

As an unbeliever, you were no real threat to the enemy, so he was content to just let you follow your own evil desires and to basically leave you alone. But after you were reborn, you instantly became a threat to him and his kingdom. The devil most likely began his attack against you with very subtle suggestions, and before you knew it, you were doubting your salvation and slipping back to your old sinning habits. Fortunately, as you grew in God's grace, you were gradually able to renew your mind and recognize and resist the devil's tactics.

Once reconciliation is realized and the city church begins to advance to develop its strategy to win back the city, one of the enemy's tactics will be to keep it divided. A divided church is no real threat to him, but when the city church achieves reconciliation and is on the way towards real unity of the faith, it poses a *major* threat to him. You can just imagine what the enemy will do. He will wait for the opportune time and slip in subtle suggestions to bring about divisiveness. He will be very aggressive with this because unity is such a huge threat to him.

In order to maintain this newfound reconciliation, you must do the same things you would recommend to a new convert:

- Become involved in a small cell or support group.
- Attend large citywide leaders' meetings with unity as the overall theme.
- Stay in the Word and in prayer, recognizing what the enemy is trying to do.

At the conclusion of the initial reconciliation, small support groups of church leaders should be formed, either formally or informally, as the Holy Spirit leads. It is important that no one is left out of these. These also act as accountability groups in the area of unity and can, in the future, become accountability groups for ministry and personal holiness as well. Each group should not let any one leader fall away from the group.

Also at the conclusion of the initial reconciliation meeting, the next citywide leaders' meeting should be established. These meetings should be held monthly initially and then shifted to quarterly. The purpose of this second meeting is to establish an executive committee. Now why would you need an executive committee, you are probably asking. Because God gave you a promise: revival would follow unity. And the church needs to walk in this promise by faith. The lost are waiting, and the enemy force is as good as defeated. The window of opportunity is wide open. The executive committee is an efficient way to ensure that this happens.

Chapter 3

Uniting the Body

"If my people who are called by my name will humble themselves and pray and seek my face and turn from their wicked ways, then I will hear from heaven and will forgive their sin and heal their land." 2 CHRONICLES 7:14

"If my people . . ."

God will heal the land (or specifically, in our case, the city) *if His people* . . . Who are His people? In the context of the passage above, His people are the people of Israel and Judah: the Jews. But because of the redemptive work of Jesus, the church also became His people. The Bible refers to the church as the body of Christ:

> Even so the body is not made up of one part but of many. Now if the foot should say, "Because I am not a hand, I do not belong to the body," it would not for that reason stop being part of the body. And if the ear should say, "Because I am not an eye, I do not belong to the body," it would not for that reason stop being part of the body. If the whole body were an eye, where would the sense of hearing be? If the whole

> body were an ear, where would the sense of smell be? But in fact God has placed the parts in the body, every one of them, just as he wanted them to be. If they were all one part, where would the body be? As it is, there are many parts, but one body.
>
> The eye cannot say to the hand, "I don't need you!" And the head cannot say to the feet, "I don't need you!" On the contrary, those parts of the body that seem to be weaker are indispensable, and the parts that we think are less honorable we treat with special honor. And the parts that are unpresentable are treated with special modesty, while our presentable parts need no special treatment. But God has put the body together, giving greater honor to the parts that lacked it, so that there should be no division in the body, but that its parts should have equal concern for each other. If one part suffers, every part suffers with it; if one part is honored, every part rejoices with it. Now you are the body of Christ, and each one of you is a part of it.
>
> —1 CORINTHIANS 12:14–27

Imagine with me for a minute the picture painted in this Scripture. Imagine an arm walking around town by the fingers on its hand and an eyeball rolling up to it to greet it. Now look at that foot over there jumping around by itself. It's all rather silly, isn't it? Yet that is generally the way the church functions in most cities. Even in those cities where the congregations have united under a common banner and have started praying together (a rare occurrence, but it does happen), the arm is still unlinked to the shoulder, and the eyeball is still out of its socket. When they do come together, they are just a mass of body parts piled together with no semblance of order. But they are together, nonetheless,; and that is a critical first step.

The reason for this disconnected mass of body parts is quite elementary. The hand has said to the foot, "I have no need of you." The eye has said to the hand, "I have no need of you." The Presbyterian has said to the Lutheran, "I don't need you." The Baptist has said to the Catholic, "I don't need you; you are not a part of me." The intercessor has said to the usher, "I don't need you." The worship leader has said to the custodian, "I don't need you." The charismatic has said to the evangelical, "I don't need you." It is all just a matter of independence or self-righteousness versus humility.

"If my people who are called by my name will humble themselves . . ."

Humility is a very simple trait, but difficult to master. It is an attribute of love and simply says, "I value you more than I value myself. I know I have great value because Jesus paid a huge price to ransom me from death and destruction, but I value you even more than I value myself." Humility is quite simply love in action, so let's take a look at what love is:

> Love is patient, love is kind. It does not envy, it does not boast, it is not proud. It does not dishonor others, it is not self-seeking, it is not easily angered, it keeps no record of wrongs. Love does not delight in evil but rejoices with the truth. It always protects, always trusts, always hopes, always perseveres. Love never fails.
>
> — 1 Corinthians 13:4–8

Love is patient. Love is kind. Love does not envy. Love does not boast. Love does not say, "Baptist, I have no need of you." Love says, "Baptist, I value you more than my very life." Love says, "Nursery worker, you have great value, even more than mine as a pastor." Humility understands that God paid a great price not only for our personal salvation but also for the salvation of every other person on this planet. Therefore, we are to love every other person just as Jesus did. We are not to boast or envy. We are not to keep a record of wrongs. We are to consider every other person as a part of the body, no matter what church they go to or what ministry God has called them to. We are all colaborers with Christ; we were all baptized by one Spirit into one body.

"If my people who are called by my name will humble themselves . . ."

Humility, taking the role of a servant towards others, is what God demands in order to heal your city.

God is saying in 2 Chronicles 7:14 that the healing of your city starts with all those in the church humbling themselves and considering others in the church of equal or greater value than themselves, whether in a different denomination, a different ministry, or a different neighborhood. It starts with me; it starts with you. It starts with each person saying, "I need you; I value you" to every other person in the church. It starts with each person honoring other members of the body.

Jesus demonstrated this in John 13:5 when He washed His disciples' feet. Peter tried to stop Him, but Jesus said that if Peter did not let Him do this, he would have no part in Him; that is, he would not be part of the body. Humility, taking the role of a servant towards others, is what God demands in order to heal your city. John 13:34–35 commands us to love one another and states that the world will know us by our love, one to another within the church.

So let me be so bold as to ask, "What are you going to do about it?" Are you going to say, "That's nice" and go on reading the next paragraph and the next chapter and finish the book and put it back on the shelf? Or are you going to let it start with you and humble yourself right now under God's mighty hand? The Holy Spirit is working even now in your heart. Begin now and pray. Ask God to demonstrate humility in your life. It matters not what others have done to you—that is in God's hands. Make a quality decision right now to walk in love and consider others of greater value than yourself. Do it now:

Father, I come to You in the name of my Lord Jesus. I confess that I have wronged You by considering myself above others in Your church in this city. I have said that I don't need them. But I do, and I repent. I have even criticized others and participated in rumors about them. I repent. I repent and turn from this wicked attitude of self-righteousness and independence.

Father, I ask that You love others through me, and I commit this day to love others and to honor them even if they ridicule me and laugh at me or even beat me or kill me. I choose this day to follow Your example and to love. In the name of Jesus I pray. Amen.

"If my people who are called by my name will . . . pray . . ."

The context surrounding 2 Chronicles 7:14 seems as if the verse is out of place in the passage. Solomon had just finished building the temple, and God was saying that He had chosen it as the place for His dwelling and that His ears would be attentive to prayers offered in the place. But then He stuck verse 14 in there, saying that if it seemed as though He had left and the devil had taken over, the people were to humble themselves and pray.

Adam had committed high treason back in the Garden of Eden and had given dominion, or rulership, of this planet to Satan. God's hands were now tied because Satan had the legal right to interfere in the affairs of this world. But God still had a secret weapon: those people who were called by His name. He had a people, and He had given them a secret weapon—prayer.

God does nothing on this earth without the prayers of His saints. I know of no one who was born again without someone first praying for them. I know of nothing that God has done without prayer first paving the way. When blind Bartimaeus ran up to Jesus and cried out, "Have mercy on me!" Jesus asked him what he wanted. Bart responded that he wanted his sight. He was a beggar so he had many other needs as well, but until that day, none of them, including his sight, had been met. He asked for his sight and got his sight—nothing more. He asked for nothing else and got nothing else. Nothing in this world happens that God is responsible for unless somebody somewhere is praying for it or has prayed for it. God is not going to heal your city unless you pray for it. Prayer is God's secret weapon and the only avenue against the devil's activities. But how are we to pray?

> "Have faith in God," Jesus answered. "Truly I tell you, if anyone says to this mountain, 'Go, throw yourself into the sea,' and does not doubt in their heart but believes that what they say will happen, it will be done for them. Therefore I tell you, whatever you ask for in prayer, believe that you have received it, and it will be yours."
> —Mark 11:22–23

> You may ask me for anything in my name, and I will do it.
> —John 14:14

These are pretty bold statements that Jesus is making. They become even bolder when we translate the word *ask* as it was meant to be translated. The word actually means to make a demand upon, as a right or privilege. Jesus has bought our righteousness, becoming our righteousness for us, and we have been made to sit with Him at the right hand of God (the traditional place of authority) in heavenly places, far above all authorities in heavenly realms and above every name that can be named. Jesus is basically saying that we are to make a demand upon, or declare with our mouths, whatever we want. And what we want here is for Jesus to be Lord over our city. We want to kick the defeated, trespassing devil out, and we want Jesus to be Lord over our city. So what we pray is really quite simple:

> *Devil, in the mighty and glorious name of Jesus, whose I am and whom I serve, I bind you and kick you out of my city* (call it by name), *and I declare that Jesus is Lord over my city* (call it by name). *Lord, I pray for righteousness to reign in my city, and I loose it here in Jesus' name.*

When we pray a prayer like this, in accordance with Matthew 18:18, we are binding the devil's activities here on earth as they are bound in heaven, and we are loosing the reign of righteousness as it is in heaven.

In the same manner, begin to pray for individual people, because no one, absolutely no one, gets born again unless they are prayed for. Begin to pray for the establishment of leadership to bring about and lead this great battle against the entrenched foe. Once the network of leadership is established, pray for those people regularly. Begin to pray for the body to become one, for each part to recognize the role that it must play within the body of Christ.

> Again, truly I tell you that if two of you on earth agree about anything they ask for, it will be done for them by my Father in heaven.
>
> —Matthew 18:19

Begin to ask the Lord to help you find those who have a like burden for your city. Seek them out, and then gather together with them to pray. The Bible says that one can put a thousand to flight, but two can put ten thousand to flight. The prayer of agreement as described in Matthew 18:19 uses this principle. Simply pray as you do privately, but pray in agreement together.

> What good is it, my brothers and sisters, if someone claims to have faith but has no deeds? Can such faith save them? Suppose a brother or a sister is without clothes and daily food. If one of you says to them, "Go in peace; keep warm and well fed," but does nothing about their physical needs, what good is it? In the same way, faith by itself, if it is not accompanied by action, is dead.
>
> But someone will say, "You have faith; I have deeds."
>
> Show me your faith without deeds, and I will show you my faith by my deeds. You believe that there is one God. Good! Even the demons believe that—and shudder.
>
> You foolish person, do you want evidence that faith without deeds is useless? Was not our father Abraham considered righteous for what he did when he offered his son Isaac on the altar? You see that his faith and his actions were working together, and his faith was made complete by what he did. And the scripture was fulfilled that says, "Abraham believed God, and it was credited to him as righteousness," and he was called God's friend. You see that a person is considered righteous by what they do and not by faith alone.
>
> In the same way, was not even Rahab the prostitute considered righteous for what she did when she gave lodging to the spies and sent them off in a different direction? As the body without the spirit is dead, so faith without deeds is dead.
>
> —James 2:14–26

God got this book into your hands for a reason and placed a burden upon your heart for a reason. What has He called you to do?

Obviously, our prayers need to be prayers of faith. They won't accomplish much if they are not. James, in the above passage, actually refers to prayers as faith, saying that some have faith and some have deeds. Having faith in this context implies that some people of faith just pray and leave the doing to those that "do." James says we should not do this. If we pray, we are also to do. So when you pray, also ask God to show you what to do. And don't do unless that doing stems from prayer and faith.

God got this book into your hands for a reason and placed a burden upon your heart for a reason. What has He called you to do? Are you to organize a prayer cell? Perhaps you are to develop the special evangelistic children's program that is required. Perhaps your special gift lies in electronics and sound. You are a part of the body of Christ in the city. In faith begin to act like it and walk in it.

> Live in me. Make your home in me just as I do in you. In the same way that a branch can't bear grapes by itself but only by being joined to the vine, you can't bear fruit unless you are joined with me.
>
> —John 15:4, MSG

> I am the Vine; you are the branches. Whoever lives in Me and I in him bears much (abundant) fruit. However, apart from Me [cut off from vital union with Me] you can do nothing. If a person does not dwell in Me, he is thrown out like a [broken-off] branch, and withers; such branches are gathered up and thrown into the fire, and they are burned.
>
> —John 15:5–6, AMP

This is love for God: To obey His commands.
—1 JOHN 3:5

Anyone who runs ahead . . . does not have God.
—2 JOHN 9

"If my people who are called by my name will . . . seek my face . . ."

Our commander-in-chief of this offensive against the devil in our city is Jesus. We absolutely must get our marching orders from Him. The only way to do this is by seeking His face. Seeking His face simply means that we enter His presence in prayer by faith to hear from Him. This is a God-breathed strategy that needs audiences with the top general (Jesus) to develop the corresponding tactics. Everyone involved in this strategic initiative needs to seek His face, to enter into His presence, and receive the orders. We cannot do this on our own, in our own strength, with our own ideas.

Many times God gives us a ministry to do. We respond and God anoints it, and it produces much fruit. It becomes so fruitful, in fact, that we start to spend more time on the ministry at the expense of our devotional time with Him. When this happens, more often than not the ministry begins to become "ours" and gradually loses its anointing. The anointing evaporates so slowly that we don't even realize it is happening. It's kind of like the motivational frog story: It's been said the best way to cook a frog is to fill a pot with cold water, put the frog in the water, and slowly turn up the heat. The frog gets comfortable and doesn't try to jump out and is eventually cooked to death. We must seek God's face and keep on seeking His face. We must remain vitally connected to Him.

We must also not run ahead of God. God may be showing you something that He has in mind so that you can properly prepare yourself in prayer and maybe study to do it. He also may be showing you something to pray into existence; it may not be something for you to actually do. But then again, God may be calling you to do it. Take the time to properly discern what God is telling you and what your part is in response.

WITHOUT ABIDING IN HIM, WITHOUT CONTINUALLY SEEKING HIS FACE AND COMMUNING WITH HIM, WE CAN DO NOTHING!!

"If my people who are called by my name will . . . turn from their wicked ways . . ."

In chapter 1, we talked about the wicked things presently in your city. Yes, those are wicked ways. But in the context of 2 Chronicles 7:14, what are wicked ways? Well, in this context, anything that is not God's way is a wicked way. We have already touched on four of them in this chapter alone: (1) original sin, (2) lack of love and humility, (3) failure to pray, and (4) failure to seek His face. That is a good start, but to understand the topic more fully, we also must understand exactly what God's ways are.

A lot is at stake here. God requires us to turn from those wicked ways to His ways before He will heal your city. And it is not the nonbeliever that He is calling to do this. It is the believer—you. God expects us to know what His ways are so that we can turn from the wicked ways to His ways. The only way to know His ways is through discipleship. And sadly, the church as a whole has fallen short of really developing true disciples.

But there is hope; there is a solution, and it is free of charge. The Fruitful Disciple Series (http://FruitfulDisciple.com) systematically takes believers through the process of learning God's ways and precepts. If you apply yourself to learn and complete this course, you will know the basics of God's ways and will be able to turn from wicked ways to

His ways. Please do *something* to discern God's ways so that you can fulfill this requirement and permit God to move in your city.

God is saying in 2 Chronicles 7:14 that the healing of your city starts with each person in the church humbling themselves and considering others in the church of equal or greater value than themselves, whether in a different denomination or a different ministry, or a different neighborhood. The church is then to pray and seek His face, privately and corporately, and turn from its wicked ways. The result of fulfilling these four conditions is unity within the body of Christ. In chapter 2, we discussed the promise of Psalm 133, that God commands His blessing of revival upon a city where the brothers dwell together in unity. Application of the principles of 2 Chronicles 7:14—true and total application, that is—brings the church together in unity and allows God to send the blessing of revival for us to walk in by faith.

Concerts of Prayer

Practically, though, how do we bring this church-body unity about? Back in the 1980s, God used a man named David Bryant to form and promote Concerts of Prayer. These were city church wide events based on the work of Jonathan Edwards in the eighteenth century. Within the framework of the event are 7 Rs: (1) rejoice, (2) repent, (3) resist, (4) restore, (5) release, (6) receive, and (7) recommit. This is an excellent method for bringing the church together in unity, but it must be preceded by weeks of preparation from the pulpit. It also must be preceded by unity among the leadership.

As we develop in both Chapters 4 and 5 of this book, you will see that these Concerts of Prayer, are critical to the overall strategy of the strategic initiative for your city, But these CoP's take on a slightly different flavor in this initiative. The first event focuses primarily on repentance, reconciliation, and unity, though the other elements are not left out. The purpose of this first event must be to develop unity and holiness in the citywide church. Every effort must be made to get every born-again believer to attend. This is a big undertaking, but fortunately, Mr. Bryant has developed a guide to help. Currently, the Concerts of Prayer guide is free, and you can download it at http://www.proclaimhope.org/content/TogetherInHope.

If everyone is moving forward together, then success takes care of itself.—HENRY FORD

Chapter 4

The Strategic Initiative

We said in chapter 1 that the battle to take your city back from the spiritual forces of wickedness will require a strategy and a concerted effort, and we discussed the military principles to apply in order to do so effectively. In chapter 2, we discovered that God has provided a mighty weapon in Psalm 133: unity. As the church leaders unite, they sign a pledge of unity and a declaration of independence from and war against the enemy, thus providing a clear objective for the strategic initiative. Chapter 3 began the process of uniting the body of Christ within the city.

It is now time to provide some substance to your city's strategic initiative by developing the unity of command that is required to win back your city. The basic framework suggested contains several distinct elements: (1) unity, (2) church preparation, (3) prayer, (4) media blitz, (5) radical and life-changing IMPACT events, and (6) pursuit and follow-up. Let's look at these one at a time.

Unity

The degree to which your city will be mobilized and subsequently won to Christ is directly proportional to and wholly dependent upon the degree to which the church leadership in your city links together in a common vision. This is where you both start and finish in bringing revival to your city.

The first step in city revival is a meeting with *all* pastors in the city, as we discussed in chapter 2. This meeting is primarily a time of repentance, reconciliation, and unity. Denominational differences will of course remain. The pastors must, however, be able to unite under a common banner to win the city for Christ. Respect for each of the pastors' individual callings, denominational worship styles, and theological stands must exist.

This first meeting then develops into a bimonthly, city-wide pastors' participatory board and monthly executive-council sessions and prayer meetings. The pastors are responsible for lifting up in prayer all city officials and key influential persons and reclaiming the gates of the city. The pastors formulate policy and pray for all team leaders.

This unity building and development is critical to the success of revival in your city. There is a key scriptural principle at work here. Without it, the revival will see only minimal results.

Church Preparation

"*If my people*, who are called by my name, will humble themselves and pray and seek my face and turn from their wicked ways, then will I hear from heaven and will forgive their sin and will heal their land" (2 Chron. 7:14, emphasis added). *The condition and actions of the church are critical to achieving true revival in your city*. This book devotes an entire chapter to this topic. Joel 2, starting with verse 12, outlines principles similar to what we find in 2 Chronicles, as do numerous other scriptures.

This phase of preparation starts with a citywide church gathering (can be a Concert of Prayer) approximately seven months prior to the IMPACT events. This is sometimes called a rally, for there is certainly cause for celebration: God is going to do something mighty in your city. But there is a cost that is described in the above scripture from 2 Chronicles. God demands humility, holiness, and prayer on the part of His people. The scripture in Joel is even more descriptive of God's demands.

So this meeting, while being a cause for celebration, is also a sacred assembly where hearts are rent. Note that as a result of this preparation, Joel says that God will send His latter rain. This has profound and dramatic implications for the upcoming IMPACT events. This initial church gathering is followed by monthly citywide Concerts of Prayer and weekly messages from the pulpit.

Prayer

Imagine the impact of Christians from every denomination meeting in neighborhood cells to pray for their neighborhood and city. It should send chills down your spine just to think of it. The enemy's strongholds are demolished as Christians pray for their neighbors. This is the air attack that must precede the coming ground invasion.

During the seventh months prior to the IMPACT events, families in the church fill out cards indicating their willingness to pray for their neighborhoods. The information on those cards is then input into a computer-mapping program, and neighborhood prayer cells are developed. These cells meet regularly to pray for individuals *by name* in their neighborhoods. They also conduct prayer walks throughout their neighborhoods.

In the last month before the IMPACT events, these cells put feet to their prayers by distributing door-hanger advertisements. The individual cell members then develop a list of ten people that they will specifically and continually pray for over the coming month. One week before the IMPACT events, the cell members will, in a very easy, unthreatening way, invite these ten people to go with them to one of the upcoming events. Most of these people will already know quite a bit about the events because of the accompanying media blitz. Their resistance will also be diminished by the massive prayer campaign and unity of the church.

During the entire seven-month campaign, intercessors are lifting up this effort 24/7 from every church in the city.

Media Blitz

Just prior to the IMPACT events, a massive media campaign is launched. This should include every available form of media in your community. Put the money where it will produce the most results. On radio, use the drive-home times. On TV, use the evening news. Use the front section of the local newspaper. This media blitz should be designed to impact the culture of every group segment in your city.

Radical and Life-Changing IMPACT Events

These will be radical! Christianity is not some wimpy religion whose relevancy is past. It is a dramatic and vital relationship with the creator of the universe. Present the gospel in this way. How would Jesus relate to your teenagers? How would He relate to your culture groups? Based on the way He did it in the Gospels, He would dramatically relate in meaningful, relevant ways. That is the way you are going to do it too. You will provide separate and individually developed events for each age and ethnic culture in your city.

You can expect signs and wonders, healings and deliverances to follow the message, in accordance with the Word of God, as God is allowed to minister to the people He loves. God is going to do this as a result of the unity and love you have shown and because of the rending of your hearts. You can simply expect these things to happen because God is God and He loves to do amazing things. By the way, IMPACT stands for Invasion Ministries Producing Actual Community Transformation as opposed to CRUSADE, which can be defined as Costly, Repetitious, Uninspiring, Systematic Approaches Delivered Everywhere.

Pursuit and Follow-Up

Throughout the Old Testament, you can repeatedly see God ordering His warriors to pursue the enemy in order to completely destroy their ability to regain a foothold. When this was not accomplished, the result was fatal. It is a key principle of war, any war. Follow-through is essential in batting, golf, tennis, etc. Pursuit is essentially following through and refusing to compromise thereby regiving gained ground.

Revival is not meant to be confined to a few select people who stand on platforms; revival is meant to revitalize a people who will operate in the anointing. So how do you do this in your city? For the most part, it is doing the same things that were done to effect revival in the city itself in the first place. Unity among the church leaders *must* continue. This is critical and most often is the place where Satan will begin to regain lost ground. The leaders should strategize future events for the city, and the pastors should develop a strategy for periodically preaching the same themes in order to break other strongholds that remain in the city and to further develop the churches under their charges.

Prayer cells, too, must continue. These are essential in the developing of new Christians and praying in those that have not yet made a decision for Christ. And finally, discipleship is critical. Consider promoting the Fruitful Disciple Series, where from the comfort of their own homes, both new converts and more mature believers can learn what it means to be a disciple of our Lord.

The Team

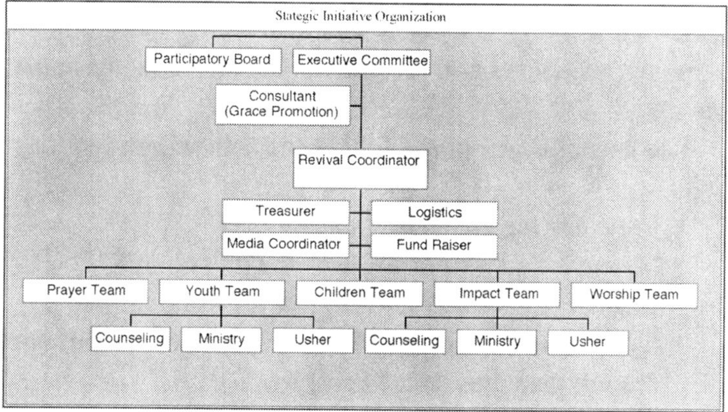

The Participatory Board

When the leaders of the church in your city gather in the initial reconciliation meeting, they form a group of united leaders that collectively form what is called the *participatory board*. This group of people are the "shareholders" of the offensive to be waged against your entrenched foe. They are the ones who sign the pledge and declaration. In many cases, these individual leaders may number in the hundreds for a given citywide church. This body needs to meet at least once more after the initial meeting to confirm the general framework of the strategic initiative. The framework described above is strongly suggested.

Even though the participatory board is united in its desire, it is too large to govern the offensive as the church walks forward by faith. The participatory board thus selects an *executive council* to carry out the strategic initiative. *The participatory board must be unified in this selection.* The participatory board must empower the executive council to perform the functions outlined below, and each participatory-board member must wholeheartedly support each executive-council member. The participatory board should ideally meet every couple of months during the campaign to remain connected and receive updates from the executive council.

The participatory board fulfills the following functions:

- Prays for the city leadership
- Maintains a spirit of unity in the city church
- Lifts the entire city and revival effort up in prayer
- Develops messages from preaching themes that each church preaches concurrently

The Executive Council

The executive council consists of key spiritual leaders from the various churches in the city in whose hearts God has placed a burning passion for winning their city. This should be a team of no more than a dozen (preferably even less) individual leaders who operate in complete unity. If one single leader opposes an action, then that action is not pursued. The council prays for unity, expects it, and gets it. The executive council meets at least monthly, and its function is to develop and govern the strategy for winning the city to Christ. Basic strategy from this book should be used, but it must be refined by the executive council to match the requirements of each individual city.

The executive council is responsible for the following functions:

- Selecting a revival coordinator (RC)
- Confirming each of the team leads proposed by the RC
- Developing the strategy
- Praying for the city's leadership
- Maintaining a spirit of unity in the city church
- Lifting the entire city and revival effort up in prayer
- Developing preaching themes that each church preaches concurrently

The Revival Coordinator (RC)

The revival coordinator is selected by the executive council and becomes a member of it. This is the key person in your city who will orchestrate the revival. While this person may be an ordained minister, it is often best that this person be an experienced Christian businessperson or entrepreneur who is wholly devoted to the Lord and with a passion for revival. This position will become a nearly full-time position and will require exceptional organizational skills and the ability to effectively deal with people, especially volunteers.

The revival coordinator closely follows the plan and strategy established by the executive council and ensures that each task is completed on time and that each team has the resources it needs. The revival coordinator also recruits leaders for each of the teams and receives confirmation of each leader from the executive council.

The Finance Team (Treasurer)

There is no doubt about it; this is going to cost money. Financially, consider this an investment that will eventually dramatically increase the church budget of every congregation in the city. Establish an independent bank account to pay all expenses. The treasurer will pay all bills from this account. The treasurer should be an accountant or experienced bookkeeper.

All necessary finances must be raised prior to any activity. In this way, the teams can focus on the needs of the people, not on paying bills. No offerings should be taken at any of the IMPACT events; rather, offerings should be taken at the Concerts of Prayer and special offerings taken at your churches for this purpose.

A typical target budget might be fifty dollars per attending person at each church. With this as a guide, a church with an average of two hundred people in attendance on a typical Sunday would contribute ten thousand dollars. After the budget is developed from input from each of the teams, you may have to adjust this contribution, but there are other possible sources of income as well. There are always key Christian businesspeople in the community who would love to get behind an event of this nature. Invite them to a luncheon during the fund-raising phase and solicit their financial involvement.

The Prayer Team

The prayer-team lead should be a person with leadership experience in cell groups, strong organizational skills, and computer literacy. This person will lead a group of people to establish neighborhood prayer cells and will provide them with a structure for their prayer meetings. The prayer-team lead also develops a corps of intercessors. This prayer effort is detailed in chapter 6.

The Worship Team

This person has the responsibility to create an atmosphere that will usher in the presence of God in each of the events staged during this revival process, including the Concerts of Prayer, the participatory-board meetings, and the executive-council meetings. The worship team needs to be able to usher in the presence of God by itself in a setting of unbelief. The worship leader must also set the tone of the meetings, creating an atmosphere of expectancy on the part of the congregation. The team leader must be a worship leader capable of doing this.

This leader will be responsible for the following:

1. Assembling local singers from across denominational lines for a worship team and choir
2. Bringing together local musical talent for the revival band
3. Assisting the logistics team in securing a quality sound system to effectively lead the worship
4. Working with the youth team to develop a worship atmosphere relevant to the local youth culture

The Logistics Team

This team leader is responsible for obtaining the facilities and equipment necessary for each of the events, including the Concerts of Prayer. The logistics team aids each of the event teams in preparing the facilities for the event and coordinates access to the facility. This team is responsible for obtaining required sound, lighting, and sanitary facilities. Each event team will establish its requirements early in the process (seven months prior to the IMPACT events) to aid in the selection of facilities.

The following should be solidified early:

1. An auditorium for the adult IMPACT events with a nearby area for the children's IMPACT events
2. A facility for the youth/college IMPACT events as specified by that team
3. High-quality sound and video equipment, as well as qualified technicians
4. Adequate ministry area to accommodate altar ministry, salvations, and prayer for miracles at the Concerts of Prayer as well as at IMPACT events
5. A separate room for each IMPACT event for counseling of new believers

A separate room for the evangelist and ministry team for prayer and preparation is needed for all major events.

Media Team Leader

The media team is responsible for maximizing the media exposure of the upcoming IMPACT events. This effort is detailed in chapter 7. You may contact Grace Promotion (Gracepromotion.org) for a marketing packet that can be easily tailored to the needs of your community.

The IMPACT Team Leader

The IMPACT team leader coordinates all aspects of the IMPACT events for adults. This team is sometimes subdivided into the following teams: counselors, ushers/security, stage crew, technical (logistics sometimes handles this), and ministry, described below.

Ushers/Security

Recruit ushers six weeks prior to the outreach events, and select them one month prior to the events. You will need approximately fifteen ushers for each one thousand attendees. Conduct a pre-outreach meeting to acquaint ushers with their duties. They should familiarize themselves with their designated areas and be given instruction on how to deal with challenging situations such as crying babies, outbursts, or disruptions of any kind.

Prepare ushers for these other duties as well:

1. Making sure doors are opened one hour before the event
2. Patrolling the halls and lobbies at appropriate intervals (keep hallways vacant)
3. Giving particular attention to unattended children or youth

All ushers should arrive fifteen minutes before the building opens, or one hour and fifteen minutes before the meeting begins.

Counselors

Recruit counselors six weeks prior to the outreach events, and select them one month prior to the events. Conduct a pre-outreach meeting to acquaint counselors with their duties. They should:

1. Know how to bring a person to new life in Christ
2. Know how to help a person in an reaffirmation of faith in Christ

3. Know how to help a person identify the healing miracle necessary and pray for a completion of that miracle if necessary

Ministry

This group of people is composed of experienced Christians who have previously worked in the area of miracles. A number of this group should be full-time ministers. These people work on the sidelines, assisting the evangelists as miracles start to flow (expect God to do this because unity will bring His presence). Their responsibilities include the following:

1. Assisting the evangelist to identify miracles that occur by interviewing people who recognize healing in their bodies
2. Assisting people at the altar to secure God's touch in their lives

Youth Team Leader

The youth team coordinates all aspects of the youth IMPACT events. The youth team is similar in structure but not in content to the IMPACT team for adults, and like that team, it is sometimes subdivided into smaller teams. The youth team creates an exciting, powerful atmosphere that draws youth to the events. The atmosphere is radical in nature and relates to the local youth culture.

The youth team leader should be empowered to flow as the Holy Spirit directs to radically impact the youth culture of your city. The RC and executive council should support and advise rather than restrain this team.

The Children's Team Leader

The children's team is made up of individuals who have a burden for the young and a desire to see them come to a relationship with Jesus. This team is composed of representatives from the city who work with children. Over a period of months, they will prepare a very unique program for children that will provide action and excitement and present the gospel in a dramatic way that is relevant to the children's culture of your city. The children's meetings will be held concurrently with a number of the adult meetings and at the same facility. Also prepare for independent events for children as the Holy Spirit directs and gives creative ideas.

Chapter 5

Boot Camp: Preparing the Church

Imagine a flood of new converts that outnumber the current church body three or four to one, or maybe even ten to one. Imagine the opening of new doors to minister to the unredeemed and sick. This is all a very good thing, but are you ready for it? Is the church ready? As you ponder this dilemma, it can quickly become overwhelming. The key, however, to managing this kind of Spirit-led revival is preparation and a very systematic process.

The first church leader I ever visited in order to present the Grace Promotion strategy was immediately overwhelmed with the consequences of pursuing such a venture. Where would he put all the people? What would he do with them, even if he got them? It was an overwhelming picture for him, and he declined.

The key to surviving this type of defeatist mentality is simply proper preparation. A farmer may plant a field, expecting a harvest, but while those seeds are growing, he better be either building a barn to contain the harvest or arranging for buyers of his produce. An army cannot go into battle without preparing the troops; boot camp and perhaps some additional training may be required. Just as going into battle without preparing the troops would be disastrous, the same is true in this strategic initiative. There are two things the church needs to prepare for before launching this initiative: (1) going into battle and (2) properly handling the resulting victory.

Preparing for Battle

When a nation goes into battle, it must prepare both in material resources and in personnel resources. Ships must be built and outfitted; weapons designed, built, and deployed; and troop transports, housing, food, and armament must be obtained. In addition, troops must be recruited, trained, and developed. In like manner, the church needs to prepare for the upcoming conflict between the saints of God and the spiritual forces of wickedness.

I really like the story of Gideon found in Judges 6 and 7. Gideon's family was at the bottom of the social class of his day, and though Gideon was the ninety-pound-weakling/nerd of his family, God called him a mighty warrior! There he was, doing the most menial of tasks, threshing wheat in a winepress, when an angel appeared to him and said, "Greetings, mighty man of valor!" Gideon responded in effect, "You have got to be kidding me." Nevertheless, God got his point across, and Gideon accepted his call. But the important part for us about this story was the selection of the army.

Gideon gathered thirty-two thousand men to battle the Midianites. Then God started His selection process. God's first cut eliminated the fearful ones and reduced the army by more than two-thirds, down to ten thousand men. Then He reduced that number to the three hundred men who drank from a kneeling position rather than from a reclining position. Those who lay down to drink by lapping the water like a dog were not aware of their surroundings, but those who drank from a kneeling position maintained an alert attitude and position, ready to respond should the need arise. The kneeling position also symbolizes for us the praying warrior, the one who says the battle is the Lord's and He alone will deliver and give the victory.

The church needs to come to the point where its absolute trust is in God rather than in man or anything man can do. Each individual saint of God needs to come to this point. And that can only be achieved through discipleship. In chapter 3, we talked about the necessity of the church to learn God's ways in order to turn from its wicked ways. To come to a point of absolute trust in God, one must learn God's ways; that is, God's redemption and love for us. The Fruitful Disciple Series is a good way to do that, and it would be a very good thing if every individual in your church actually went through the series so that everyone would have the same foundation, much like what happens in boot camp.

But there must also be additional teaching specific to the needs of the strategic initiative and upcoming IMPACT events. This additional teaching should come from the pulpit and should be preached concurrently from every church. Here are a few topics that are common to most communities, but you may determine that others are necessary for your particular situation.

2 Chronicles 7:14

The application of this scripture to transforming your city was detailed in chapter 3. This needs to be expounded upon from each pulpit. It can actually be developed into a four-part series: (1) unity and love (this may require several weeks of sermons as a prelude to the first Concert of Prayer), (2) the need for prayer, (3) seeking God's face and abiding, and (4) humility.

Prayer

This could be another multipart series and is detailed in chapter 6 of this book. The messages might include the following: (1) prayer cells and blessing prayer, (2) prayers of agreement, (3) fasting (a good time for this is just before the citywide declared fast), (4) preventive prayers for leaders and individuals, and (5) bringing heaven to earth.

Witnessing

This might be better offered as a workshop where practical application can take place. This capability will need to be developed as the barriers preventing salvation are broken down and people become more receptive. Many will not need to wait until the IMPACT events to experience redemption, so the church needs to be ready to bring them in.

In addition to preparing its people for battle, the church must make arrangements for the necessary material resources. This was discussed in the preceding chapter and will be further examined in chapter 8. Money needs to be raised. Worship teams need to be organized and developed. Children's events need to be planned. Youth events need to be planned. Facilities need to be retained. Many, many things involving the church need to be done. However, preparing the individual church members is the most critical step and can be accomplished by using the suggestions for sermon series and the Fruitful Disciple Series.

Preparing for Victory

It is one thing to go into battle. It is quite another to know what to do after victory is won. In fact, next to developing unity, preparing for victory is probably the hardest part of the process. You have worked hard to win your city, and in great anticipation of what you believed God was going to do, you prepared. It was truly exciting to see God move in spectacular ways. It was wonderful. But now, like cleaning the dishes after a fantastic meal or tidying the house after a party, the hard part comes.

Before the IMPACT events, the city was run by a despot demon appointed by the devil himself. Now he is no longer present, and people do not know what to do. They figure they should go to church, but they don't seem to fit anywhere, both figuratively and physically. The church suddenly has a multitude of baby Christians on its hands and no bassinettes to put them in.

The church includes both physical structures and the community of believers. You must prepare both for this coming flood of new converts. Dealing with the space issue is crucial because people by their very natures (and currently they only have their old natures to refer to) do not go where they are not accepted. Squeezing people into a crowded sanctuary immediately makes people feel unappreciated and not valued.

You can deal with this problem in several ways or maybe in a combination of ways. You could schedule more services. If you currently have one service and your sanctuary is full for it, after the IMPACT events you may need to offer three or four services. Another option is to temporarily rent a larger space for worship, or you could actually welcome new church planters into your community to assume some of the spiritual load. Another thing to remember is that you will most probably need to hire new support staff. Get ready for all these physical changes and make plans for them, but don't actually do anything drastic like building a new building until the dust settles and you find out what your needs are—that is, of course, unless God tells you to do something drastic to prepare for the victory.

Dealing with your current church body and getting them ready for dealing with the new converts probably presents the greatest challenge. Your current parishioners have among them both leaders and followers. They all will need to stretch. The leaders will need to become leaders of more and will also have to teach the followers how to lead. You will need more leaders to become mentors, or spiritual parents, for all those new babies, so practically every current disciple will have to become a mentor to several of the new converts. To do so, they first must become true fruitful disciples themselves.

Each church in your community is probably like every other church in the world. Most churches have some parishioners who just come to church out of a sense of duty, some who come for the fellowship or business contacts, and still others who come for actual discipleship and growing in the Lord and serving Him. Somehow, before the revival flood hits, most of the congregants need to be transformed into the latter category. Again—and I know I am sounding like a broken record—the Fruitful Disciple Series, particularly the classroom material, can help tremendously to prepare your congregation. You will probably want the classroom materials so that actual growth can be monitored before the discipling of newly redeemed converts is entrusted to unknowns.

> *Imagine churches helping each other to meet the physical needs of their growth.*

Like the battle-preparatory period, the victory-preparatory period can also benefit from a series of pulpit messages preached concurrently throughout the city church. A series on leadership and mentorship would be very beneficial. Another series on intimacy with God and abiding would be very fruitful. You may also want to begin preparing leaders of home cell groups, because this is where real ministry to new believers will take place.

A New, Fresh Idea

Back in chapter 2, we saw how the leaders of the city church gathered together and declared unity in their city and in the war against the spiritual forces of darkness. Then in chapter 3, we saw the church gathering in unity and starting to consider members of other churches as necessary for the health of the entire city church. Now suppose, just suppose, that this new problem of a massive influx of newly redeemed converts was handled and solved by this new city church instead of individually by each church. I believe a completely new city life can be created when brothers do, in fact, dwell together in unity.

Imagine cell groups formed with members from various church bodies. Imagine churches helping each other to meet the physical needs of their growth. The church cannot really control exactly where the new converts are going to choose to settle, but they can dedicate themselves to supporting wherever that might be. This is love in action and the way church life is meant to be lived.

Chapter 6

The Air Attack: Strategic Prayer

In most military conflicts, an air attack precedes the actual ground battle. This air attack serves to soften the enemy forces and make it easier for the ground forces. In ancient times, this air attack was typically in the form of archers and artillery such as the catapult and trebuchet. Opposing forces would use these tools to safely conduct the battle from a distance. Following the invention of gunpowder, both land-based and fleet-based cannons were used in place of the ancient forms of artillery. While long-range large guns are still used, especially from ships, aircraft now provide the primary form of air attack.

Strategically, bombing raids are used to weaken the opposing force prior to committing land-based forces to the confrontation. Once the land-based forces move in, tactical air attacks are called in only as needed to support those ground troops prior to confronting a specific opposing force. In the spiritual realm, prayer is our air-attack weapon. The purpose of prayer is obviously to get God involved in the conflict. But what we are after is strategic prayer—prayer that will actually work in this battle to take back our city.

We can use Jesus' model of prayer as used in His ministry, and we can liken His ministry to the strategic offensive we are taking. The Bible states that the reason Jesus came was to destroy the works of the devil, and this is what we are doing as we work to take our city back from the enemy. For our purposes, Jesus' strategic offensive is best outlined in the Gospel of Luke, starting in chapter 3. [2]

John the Baptist and Jesus were cousins. In fact, their mothers were uniquely bonded in the extraordinary miraculous pregnancy that each of the women experienced. Both angels and the Holy Spirit confirmed whom each of them was carrying. Even in the womb, the babies recognized each other. They were cousins, and because the mothers were close, the boys were probably close as well. Once John started his ministry, he knew what he was about and he knew what Jesus was about, and he knew he was called to prepare His way.

At the baptism of Jesus, John declared just who Jesus was: "Behold the Lamb of God that takes away the sins of the world." Then God the Father got involved and declared, "You are My Son, whom I love; in You I am well pleased." Though John audibly heard the words, it is not clear that the crowd actually heard them. Since John already knew who Jesus was and the statement from the Father served no purpose for the crowd at this stage in Jesus' ministry, this declaration was in effect a declaration of war. God was placing the devil on notice that here was the sinless one who had come to crush his head. And the devil sat up and took notice.

Then we read how the Holy Spirit led Jesus into the desert, where He was tempted by the devil. Jesus won that first skirmish, and He came out of the desert in the power of the Holy Spirit. The devil went away for a while, waiting for a more opportune time to trip Him up.

It didn't take long for the devil to find that more opportune time. Jesus started out great; all were amazed at the gracious words that flowed from His lips. Then suddenly the group became angry—so angry, in fact, that they wanted to stone Him and throw Him off a cliff (see Luke 4:29). Obviously, the devil was inciting this group to such an extreme level of hatred. Jesus then encountered a big-time demon that got right in His face in a very disrespectful way. Jesus clobbered him, but the devil just sent more; other Gospels name this particular group, Legion, "for we are many." Though Jesus took care of them too, He was continually hampered by demons until He changed the spiritual atmosphere.

Note that Jesus was also hampered by religious leaders, and He said in Luke 8:44 that this opposition came directly from the devil. John was imprisoned and grew discouraged. This was the same guy who had said to Jesus, "I am not worthy to untie the sandals of Your feet," but now he wondered if Jesus truly was the Savior after all. He thus sent his disciples to ask Jesus if He was the one.

Then the devil tried to kill Jesus and His disciples on the Sea of Galilee. This storm was obviously the work of the devil, not God, because the attack came while Jesus was sleeping, and Jesus had authority over it. A little later, Satan tried to stir up the disciples. A couple of them wanted to call down fire from heaven; they expressed contempt for the crowd that Jesus was ministering to, and they even fought among themselves. Jesus eventually forbade them to preach and even stated that Peter was actually the mouthpiece of the devil. It got to the point where Jesus could not recruit any more followers, and He voiced His frustration, saying, "O unbelieving and perverse generation, how long shall I stay with you and put up with you?" (Luke 9:41).

In Luke 10, however, the tide changed; the spiritual atmosphere reversed. Now Jesus was "rejoicing greatly in the Holy Spirit" (Luke 10:21). From this point forward, He encountered only two minor demons. The religious leaders became afraid of Him, and the disciples humbly asked to be taught how to pray and to receive power to perform the tasks Jesus gave them. The multitudes now marveled and increased. When Jesus healed a blind man in Jericho, the entire town converted. There was a new atmosphere in place, and the battle turned. It was like the archers and the catapults had softened the ground resistance for Jesus. But what happened in chapter 10 to make such a difference?

Blessing prayer is the air-attack weapon of choice in our battle against your entrenched foe, and love is the key to winning your city back.

In Luke 10, Jesus appointed seventy-two followers and sent them out two by two to the places He planned to go. He instructed them to first speak peace to the house where they were staying. This was notably different from what He had told the Twelve to do previously. In effect, He was saying to the seventy-two, "Pray a blessing on each house. Love the people first and foremost."

As these seventy-two were blessing the people in the towns Jesus would be visiting, Jesus saw Satan fall from heaven like a lightning bolt. Satan didn't just fall to the ground by the force of gravity, he was forced from his place of authority at the speed of light. Those prayers of blessing were the effective air attack that paved the way for Jesus to come in and minister unhindered. Prayers of blessing are love in action, and against such there is no law. Love defeats the devil at every turn. He has nothing that can effectively fight against it.

Blessing prayer is the air-attack weapon of choice in your battle against our entrenched foe, and love is the key to winning your city back. But it is important to have a plan, a battle plan, if you will. Just how do you go about using this weapon and incorporating it into the battle plan? Below are described several other principles regarding prayer as outlined in the Word of God in order to maximize the effectiveness of this weapon.

Biblical Principle 1: The Prayer of Agreement

Notice in Luke 10 that Jesus sent the disciples out two by two. He was using the age-old biblical principle that one can put a thousand to flight, but two can put ten thousand to flight. Jesus amplified this principle in Matthew 18:19–20:

> Again, truly I tell you that if two of you on earth agree about anything they ask for, it will be done for them by my Father in heaven. For where two or three gather in my name, there am I with them.

At every opportunity, we need to use this principle of agreement to multiply the prayer power of the saints. This is not to diminish the importance to also pray often personally, by ourselves. After all, one can still put a thousand to flight, and it is not always possible to physically gather together with other believers.

Biblical Principle 2: Fasting

There are huge misconceptions about fasting. This is a practice that I have personally devoted much time to and have found it extremely powerful, and also on some occasions it has been a complete waste of time. It all depended on my motivation going into it and how I did it.

Many people view fasting as eating fish instead of beef on Friday. Others view fasting as a "Daniel fast" or laying off rich foods. Some people fast by skipping one meal a day for several days, and others fast by eating only ice cream. Still others fast from recreation, such as watching TV. For me personally, only one kind of fasting works all the time and carries with it incredible power. It is a declared full fast, meaning the eating of no food at all (just plenty of water), and it is done for a specific purpose:

> "Why have we fasted," they say, "and you have not seen it? Why have we humbled ourselves, and you have not noticed?"
>
> Yet on the day of your fasting, you do as you please and exploit all your workers. Your fasting ends in quarreling and strife, and in striking each other with wicked fists. You cannot fast as you do today and expect your voice to be heard on high. Is this the kind of fast I have chosen, only a day for people to humble themselves? Is it only for bowing one's head like a reed and for lying in sackcloth and ashes? Is that what you call a fast, a day acceptable to the LORD?
>
> *Is not this the kind of fasting I have chosen: to loose the chains of injustice and untie the cords of the yoke, to set the oppressed free and break every yoke?*
>
> —Isaiah 58:3–6, emphasis added

This is the kind of fasting Jesus did in the wilderness. He didn't go out there to discover His ministry, to identify the strategy God wanted Him to follow, or even to seek an anointing on His life. He had all those things already. This fast was so that the deaf could hear, the blind could see, the lame could walk, the dead could be raised, the lepers could be cured, and the good news could be preached to the poor. It was for others and was a full fast for forty days straight. (It is also the type of fasting that birthed this book.)

This does not mean your fast has to last forty days (there was a physiological reason, however, for the forty days). It should be for whatever length of time God leads you to set. But the quoted passage above says that God does not even see fasting unless it flows from a foundation of unity and love and is done with the declared purpose to set the oppressed free and to break every yoke imposed by the devil. Fasting must flow from this foundation of love for others, not for yourself or your personal benefit.

Fasting is truly a spiritual exercise that releases an extreme degree of power. Even though the purpose of fasting should be to "untie the cords of the yoke, to set the oppressed free and break every yoke," there are also benefits reaped as a result of the practice. Once the fast is over (not during the fast), you should expect to see these benefits:

> *Then your light will break forth like the dawn and your healing will quickly appear; then your righteousness will go before you and the glory of the Lord will be your rear guard.*
> —Isaiah 58:8

True fasting is always done for others. It is not for humbling yourself before God or trying to make God notice you or your prayers. It flows from a position of unity and love and is always for the benefit of others. Fasting should be done at the personal level, small-group level, and in citywide declared fasts. Fasting is extremely powerful in its intended purpose of breaking the yoke and setting the captives free. It is another kind of blessing prayer that hugely amplifies the spoken prayer.

Biblical Principle 3: Prayer for Leaders

> I urge, then, first of all, that petitions, prayers, intercession and thanksgiving be made for all people—for kings and all

> those in authority, that we may live peaceful and quiet lives in all godliness and holiness.
> —1 TIMOTHY 2:1–2

Imagine the impact of every single person in the city praying blessing prayer over the community leaders—by name. Paul says that this leads to a quiet and peaceful life in all godliness and dignity. Note that the Scripture says "first of all." When we go to prayer, after adoration of our Lord, the first people we pray for are our community leaders.

The second group of leaders to pray for encompasses those in leadership positions in the church and in the strategic offensive. Pray for the pastors, teachers, evangelists, and apostles. Pray also for the revival coordinator and all the team leaders. It is vitally important to pray a hedge of protection around them each and every time you pray.

The primary mechanism the devil will employ to bring down the offensive or render it impotent will be an attempt to sway the leadership and those closest to them, especially their spouses. So pray for these leaders and their loved ones. If you are one of these leaders, ask God to give you enhanced personal discernment and spiritual conviction so that you can maintain yourself pure, holy, and in unity. You must do this to prevent the development of holes in that hedge around you that would allow the devil access to your life.

Biblical Principle 4: Bring Heaven to Earth

> Your kingdom come, your will be done, on earth as it is in heaven.
> —MATTHEW 6:10

Jesus said to pray such that you bring God's will as it is in heaven down to earth where we are. So as you pray, picture what is and what is not in heaven. There is love in heaven. There is joy in heaven. There is blessing in heaven. There is no sickness in heaven. There are no devils in heaven. All those in heaven are believers. Pray such that you bring heaven to earth.

Jesus discussed this concept further in Matthew 18:18. He said whatever you bind on earth is bound in heaven, and whatever you loose on earth is loosed in heaven. Essentially, you can bind anything you see on earth that is not in heaven. However, ensure that you release, or loose, the corresponding countering characteristic that is in heaven to replace that which you bind. You will find that prayers of just binding without the corresponding loosing are largely ineffective.

The Air Battle Plan

Organize Your Air Force

Your air force, which is your prayer initiative, has two components: (1) the intercessors, or the bomber division, and (2) the neighborhood prayer groups, or the fighter-jet squadrons. While it is the job of every believer to intercede on a regular basis, there are those who are called specifically to intercession. These people will spend hours on their knees and even pray through the night on occasion. These intercessors are already in your city church and need to get organized and gather together to maximize the efficiency of their prayers. Intercessors are indeed special people, and they need to be called out, honored, and unified under a common banner. They need to meet regularly to share what the Holy Spirit has shown each of them and to submit a summary report to the RC.

The rank-and-file prayer warriors, which include the rest of us, also need to get organized. At the first Concert of Prayer and at each church service the following Sunday, a call should be given for all who would be willing to commit

> *Each and every person in your city is prayed for <u>by name</u> on a continual and consistent basis for a protracted period of time.*

to pray to fill out information cards providing their names, addresses, phone numbers, e-mail addresses, and other pertinent information. It should be emphasized that those filling out these cards need not have any experience whatsoever in intercession. The prayer team will train them in the principles of blessing prayer as described above. The information on these cards is entered into a database and mapping program. From this mapping, neighborhood prayer cells are formed. These cell groups meet regularly, preferably weekly, and from the cell groups the two-by-twos are formed to pray for those in the neighborhood. You might want to construct this so that the youth intercessors are organized according to the mapping program as well but separate from the adults. And don't forget the children. Because of their sincerity and purity, children make very effective prayer warriors. They typically don't question the concepts presented here as many adults do; they just understand it and do it.

You can also structure prayer cells around the workplace, but these should be secondary to the neighborhood cells. Each and every household and each and every person in that household needs to be prayed for. Each prayer cell should research the names of the people in their neighborhood so that each and every person in your city is prayed for by name on a continual and consistent basis for a protracted period of time.

Prayer Events

Numerous prayer events need to occur during the strategic initiative. I will present suggested events here in the order that they would be performed in a typical citywide strategic initiative.

The Gateways

Each city has gateways into it and a perimeter around it. These are represented both in a natural, physical way and in a spiritual, heavenly way. The enemy has controlled these gateways for a long, long time, and the city church needs to take them back. *This must be accomplished first by the church leaders in the city.* Once unity has been achieved and the declaration signed, these leaders need to gather at each of the gateways to the city as soon as possible after that initial gathering. You may want to divide the gateways among the leadership of the city church in such a way that three or four leaders are assigned to each gateway.

At each gateway, kick out (bind) the satanic guards over that gateway and loose heavenly angels to take their places. Then walk the perimeter to the next gateway, which should have been prayed over by another leadership group. As you walk this perimeter, pray blessing prayers over your city, particularly for the section of the city where you are currently located. As you walk the perimeter, imagine yourself carrying a roll of saran wrap several yards high and completely wrapping your city for God. You are essentially claiming your city back for God. This is an intensely spiritual exercise and absolutely must be accomplished, no matter how silly it may seem to you. Imagine Abraham walking around his land when God told him that everywhere he placed his feet would be his. He probably looked a bit silly too.

Leadership Prayer Rallies

The participatory board should meet periodically for two reasons: (1) to maintain unity and (2) to pray for the city. This meeting could take the form of a mini Concert of Prayer presented in a more informal fashion but strictly for the church leadership. It could, however, be expanded to include other pastoral staff who may want to participate.

Concerts of Prayer

These are massive events, and if your city is large, the events probably need to be held in an arena. You should hold these at least monthly, and the entire church should be invited. Every believer needs to make a concerted effort to attend. These corporate gatherings for the sole purpose of prayer and unity are like nuclear warheads striking the enemy stronghold above your city. After these events begin, you should be able to sense the difference in the atmosphere in your city almost immediately.

Neighborhood Prayer Walks

Like the perimeter walk performed by the leadership, these walks need to be done only once by each two-by-two team. The intent is for each team to walk the perimeter of its particular neighborhood section and wrap it with the imaginary saran wrap. This is an intensely spiritual activity and sets the geographical area apart for each team as they establish a perimeter of faith. It is important for each team to walk its perimeter at least once at the launching of its prayer activity. The team may, however, walk within this perimeter on a regular basis to pray for each and every individual residing in that area.

Neighborhood Cell-Group Meetings

The purpose of these meetings is simply to add a multiplication factor to the prayers. These meetings should start with a period of sharing what God is doing in each team, continue with some worship time, and then close with prayer for each individual. This meeting can definitely take two to three hours. You might want to periodically change the format by perhaps holding a mini prayer fair for your neighborhood.

In this event, you send out notices that you are going to be available to pray for any needs, and then you erect a canopy at a central location and pray with those who respond.

Declared Fasts

The entire church should declare a fast just prior to the IMPACT events. However, each cell pair and cell group can and should declare smaller fasts just prior to any activity that involves physical encounters with the people in their neighborhood. For example, perhaps a day-long fast is in order just before that mini prayer fair. In the IMPACT chapter, we will discuss actually inviting each person in the neighborhood to the IMPACT events. This should be preceded by a period of fasting. Fasting can be done periodically at other times as well. Use this very powerful tool to break the yoke of bondage in the lives of those you are praying for.

Jesus set the stage for His ministry by sending out the seventy-two in pairs to speak blessing prayers over the communities He was targeting. After they paved the way, it was incredibly easy for Him to minister there. He essentially had no opposition and, on the offensive, moved in with power to reach the lost. We can do the same.

---

[2] I owe a deep debt of gratitude to Beverly Jaime, Associate Pastor at Cathedral of Faith in San Jose, CA for her tutelage in the principles behind Lighthouses of Prayer, from which came these insights into Jesus' battle documented in the Gospel of Luke. Further insights came from Prayer Evangelism by Ed Silvoso, who is the founder of Harvest Evangelism. I highly recommend all of his books.

Chapter 7

Getting the Word Out: Media Blitz

The previous chapters have focused on warfare because there really is a battle going on in the heavenlies. A massive confrontation is taking place as your city soundly defeats the demonic forces arrayed against it. This is a battle against spiritual forces—against demons, not people.

When it comes to the people of your city, your strategy must now shift from the warfare mode. It must be motivated by love. We therefore turn now to take a look at effective marketing techniques because at its root, marketing is a strategy of love. Marketing, done properly, focuses on the customers and their perceptions, needs, and desires.

There are two phases to your marketing campaign, and they are presented in this chapter and the next. The first phase is focused on persuading the citizens of your city to attend the IMPACT events, which are your product. The second phase is to sell Jesus. That almost sounds degrading, "selling Jesus," but in the purest form of sales, that is precisely what you are doing. Sales is nothing more than convincing people of their need for your product, whatever it may be, and leading them through a decision-making process to expend a part of their existing life to gain it.

Evangelism *is* sales, and for too long we have spiritualized it and refused to call it such. This is largely due to our perception that sales is dirty and not worthy of the gospel. Granted, much of our current perception of sales may be warranted. When we think of sales, many of us automatically think of high-pressure car-, appliance-, or maybe insurance-sales professionals who seemingly use any tactic, ethical or otherwise, to twist our arms to purchase their products. I am not attacking these sales professionals directly; most are very ethical and well-intentioned professionals. What I am presenting is the fact that our perception of the profession has been tarnished by a few unethical people we have encountered or heard of. They have left a sour taste in our mouths, and we perceive that the entire profession is that way, when in reality it is not.

> *Marketing, done properly, focuses on the customers and their eptions, needs, and desires.*

Sales is a very noble profession that seeks to fill perceived needs in people's lives. It is really a profession of love. And evangelism is sales—pure and simple. Evangelism is convincing people of their need for Jesus and leading them through a decision-making process to relinquish their existing life to gain Him.

Let's think about the church in general for a minute and evangelism in particular. Consider that the church's mission is to make disciples of all those within its sphere of influence. Yet what are we doing to make that happen? Think about the name of your particular congregation. Is it First Baptist or maybe Saint James Lutheran? Just what does that mean to the unchurched? Does it make them want to come in and see what you have to offer? Just a thought. How about the terms *gospel* or *saved* or even *good news*? Do the unchurched know what these terms mean, and do the terms make them want what you have to offer? More than likely, no. They haven't a clue. And what's more, a large number of people within the church do not understand these terms either, because in many of the churches across our nation, the church is nothing more than a social club that goes through a ritual every Sunday morning. Though there are some exceptions, no life, no vibrancy, is the norm. There is no condemnation meant here—just a statement of fact. Within this scenario, picture yourself as one of the unchurched. Would you really want to become "churched"? Would you want the product? I would venture to say no. The facts speak for themselves.

As we approach the mission with the people of your city, we must look through the eyes of those we are trying to reach. Marketing and advertising gurus often say, "Perception is everything." Those people we are trying to reach will define our strategy to reach them just as potential customers and their perception of need always define any good marketing program. Marketing is defined as the set of all activities that contribute to building ongoing relationships with customers in order to grow a business. We need to approach our program to reach the people of your city from a marketing perspective and design it through the use of effective marketing principles.

I once started a company that designed and built post-and-beam (timber-frame) houses with thatched roofs that resembled old English cottages. It was a very novel and quaint idea that I thought people would love and flock to. Turns out they didn't. An age-old business strategy is simply to find a need (perceived or real) and fill it, and if the need does not exist, create it. I thought I would do the latter part and create that perceived need. But I was no Steve Jobs. Steve had an uncanny ability to perceive what customers will think they need before they have any idea that they do;

hence, the success of Apple. I, however, did not possess that ability.

The church often acts in much the same way that I did. We in the church have this great relationship with Jesus and with each other, and it is very real for us. But we mistakenly think that everyone else would naturally like to have the same. The truth is, however, that most other people are quite happy, or perceive that they are happy, with their lives and relationships just as they are. They perceive no need for Jesus or for the church. And remember, in marketing, perception is everything.

Chapter 6 of this book presented a prayer strategy—a massive air attack—to prepare the hearts of the citizens of our city. But like sheepdogs herding a flock of sheep into new and better pasture, we must gently and purposefully guide our fellow citizens into a paradigm shift that will alter their perceived need for Jesus. Jesus, the Good Shepherd, has prepared the pasture and the sheep, but we have the responsibility to bring them to it—and it is a great honor to do so. So let's do it correctly, with passion and purpose. Let's design a marketing program specifically for our city that will have the ultimate consequence of creating a city of life.

Our first objective is to bring the citizens of the city to the IMPACT events. Attendance at these events is our product, so to speak. If we were to hold these events tomorrow, attendance would likely be quite small because there is no perceived need to attend. We would get a few curiosity seekers, but that is essentially all.

At this point, some of you are probably protesting, "He is saying we need to brainwash the city." There are companies and organizations that do specialize in perception modification, or brainwashing, and yes, we are doing that. I will be blunt and honest—we are. However, the Bible says we are to brainwash ourselves, or renew our minds, because the world and the devil have filled our minds with false perceptions that need to be replaced with truth. So it is nothing new. But we do need to look at which perceptions we are attempting to modify in our city.

The devil has been in control of your city for decades, and his prime objective has been to blind people's perception of their need for a savior. He is the ultimate liar and deceiver, and he is the one who has created this false perception that they do not need God (the Bible calls it "blinding the eyes"). Your focus in prayer is that God would open the eyes of the people in your city to their need for a savior. And that will happen because the unity and love that have been established will break the devil's power over them. Your job now is to remove the false perception established by the enemy, and you do that through sound marketing techniques. Let me reiterate here the need for unity and love. Without these, any marketing attempts will ultimately fail because the devil's power will not yet have been broken.

The Five Ps of Marketing

All marketers have had the five basic points of marketing drilled into them. These are commonly referred to as *influence points* that relate what is being marketed to the customer. The customer is king, and all influence points relate directly back to the customer. In good marketing, everything is viewed from the customer's perspective. The five influence points of marketing are (1) product, (2) price, (3) placement, (4) promotion, and (5) people.

The Product

As previously stated, the product for our first phase of outreach is attendance at the IMPACT events, whatever they may be. At these events, each person in attendance will have the opportunity to meet Jesus. These events need to be exciting and perceived as something the customer needs or wants. We will discuss the actual events in the next chapter. The focus now is on convincing the citizens of their need to attend.

The Price

Attendance at the IMPACT events must be perceived as worth the price the customers are being asked to pay. Think about the price as perceived by the average unchurched person. Is it time away from other pursuits? Is it money? Is it the perceived result of attendance, such as having to give up a portion of their life in the process? The obstacle to overcome here is any perceived cost, whatever it may be.

The Placement

The IMPACT events must occur at a place and time that is convenient for most of the people that you want to attend. In addition, the children's events must be collocated with the adult events to make it easier for the adults.

The Promotion

There are many tools to use in the promotion of the IMPACT events. The primary purpose of these promotional tools is to shape the customer's perception of the events. This is where we will focus much of the remaining chapter.

The People

It will be obvious that the church is the organization sponsoring and promoting these events that you want the citizens to attend. Remember, people are the church, so the perception needs to be that church people love one another and love the unchurched. If this perception does not currently exist, then it needs to. Consider all the things that need to happen in order to create this perception.

Perception Promotion

A paradigm shift or perception change is best accomplished very slowly. That is why your media blitz actually starts many months ahead of the IMPACT events. It starts with planting a tiny seed. Each individual is being prayed for so that their eyes will be opened and the enemy's hold broken, so begin planting new seeds to develop that need for God in their lives. Consider a few strategically placed billboards with thought-provoking statements or questions like "Talked to God lately?" Then change it up every two to three weeks to keep interest going. Perhaps a subsequent billboard would be "God is coming to town: R U ready?" Eventually you will introduce the branding of your events as the answer to this growing need for God. This promotion campaign will gradually build to a crescendo as the IMPACT event nears. The billboard is just one example to illustrate the process. There are many other tools to use, and they are discussed below. But remember to always be people-focused in love and to be incredibly creative.

Communicating to the Whole Person

Not all advertising communicates to both the intellectual part and the emotional part of a person, But the really good ones do. Those advertisements that we remember and relate to a particular brand almost always communicate to both the intellect and emotions. In our strategic initiative, we also have a third dimension that we are communicating to, and that is the spiritual.

Each form of promotional media you use needs to be prayed over. It needs to be anointed of God to reach the unchurched people of your city. Use emotional appeals to grab attention and intellectual information to keep interest, but don't forget that the spiritual component is absolutely necessary to draw the people to your event.

Print Advertising

The bulk of all advertising is print advertising, and that is especially true in small cities. That said, the promotions market is a rapidly changing one, with web-based promotion taking over a large chunk of the market. You will need to assess how your city's culture best receives promotional media. Print advertising is still very effective, though, and it comes in many forms.

Print ads should contain the following elements:

- Headline: This is composed of large-print words that catch the eye and is usually placed at the top of the ad.
- Subhead: This optional wording provides additional information regarding the headline and usually appears in a slightly smaller size.
- Copy: This is the main text. Set a readable-sized font.
- Visual: This provides an illustration that makes a visual statement. Ads without any visuals are simply boring.
- Trademark and signature: These identify the company, usually with a logo or typed version of the company name.
- Slogan: This is optional, but its purpose is to evoke the spirit of the brand.

Great print advertising jumps off the page and grabs the reader. It is a good idea to page through publications like magazines and newspapers and notice those ads that grab you. Then do what they do.

A Note on Fonts

Fonts can be either *sans serif* or *serif*. Serif fonts have little feet on the characters. These are traditionally used to help the reader. The little serifs create an imaginary line that helps the eye follow the text. This type of font is great for body copy or wherever there are many words to read. Most major newspapers and nearly all books use this type of font for body text. Serif fonts in body copy read much faster, so where time is important, use serif. A commonly used serif font is Times New Roman. Others are Garamond and Century Schoolbook. This book is set in the Times serif font.

The sans serif font is a font without those little feet. In general, the sans serif fonts are great for catching the eye and are typically used by large publications for titles and subtitles and other places where attracting attention is important. Use of sans serif fonts in body copy, however, slows the eye down. Commonly used sans serif fonts are Arial and Helvetica, but there are many others.

Brochures and Posters

You will probably need to produce brochures and posters describing the IMPACT events. Make sure you use eye-catching visuals or, at the least, eye-catching headlines. Your brochure or poster needs to contain the following three things:

- The appeal: an enticing headline and compelling copy with a visual
- The subheads: words used to define the structure of the information on the document
- The fact base: information included for reference purposes

Brochures are generally produced as a trifold measuring $8^{1/2}$ x 11 inches and printed on heavy-paper stock. There are many quality templates found in both word-processing and page-layout programs that make it easy to design brochures.

In today's hectic schedule, many people receiving a trifold will often put it aside and look at it later. It frequently sits untouched, gathering dust, so it's best to use trifolds as a way to provide additional information. However, well-designed one-third-page brochures or cards that are printed on glossy card stock front and back are more likely to be read and produce a much greater impact. The front should present the appeal in a very eye-catching, compelling manner, while the back should provide the fact base. These can also be used as postcards or door hangers.

Tickets

While there will probably not be a charge for entry into the IMPACT events, tickets can still be a powerful tool. Giving out tickets for each member of a family shows you care and adds to the probability that they will attend. In addition to the typical "Admit One," the ticket should include the date, time, and place of the event. Tickets can also be a means of controlling attendance. Since your IMPACT events will probably go on for several days and nights, you will want to spread participation over that period. Tickets can help with this.

Billboards

The use of billboards has already been introduced as a tool to convey a thought to stimulate the perception change. That is what billboards are good for. They have to be kept short, and they have to catch the eye. You absolutely do not want to put too much on them to distract the driver. A very simple, thought-provoking message is best, or a graphic with dates is also a good option. Brand the sign with your website address so the drivers can go there to get more information when they get home.

Billboards come in two basic sizes: the poster and the bulletin. A poster is often called a 30-sheet poster and measures 21 feet 7 inches wide by 9 feet 7 inches high. It is typically used on two-lane roads or four-lane roads where the traffic is relatively slow. The bulletin billboard is much larger at 48 feet wide by 14 feet high. It is used on high-speed highways such as interstates.

Billboards may seem expensive at an average cost of $3,500 a month in the United States (plus design and printing costs), but their reach is far greater and at a lower cost per impression than radio, TV, and print ads. Be careful, though. Before you spend any money on designing and printing a billboard, check out your local ordinances. Many states do not allow billboards.

Promotional Items: Pens and T-Shirts

Pens are great as giveaways and when added to a mailing cause the recipient to actually open the envelope and perhaps read the message, especially when the message is a one-third-page brochure or card. The message on the pen should give the recipient something to remember, like the date and place for the IMPACT event. T-shirts and hats can be used to identify staff at your various events, including mini prayer events and Concerts of Prayer. They can also be used as fund-raisers and offered for sale at the Concerts of Prayer.

Broadcast Advertising

Website

As I write this, the commercial Internet is only about fifteen years old; nevertheless, its influence has grown tremendously, almost exponentially, in that time. Businesses absolutely have to have a website in order to survive, and it is becoming more and more necessary for churches to have a web presence as well. Many businesses actually sell their merchandise via the Internet, and numerous churches allow people to download podcasts of their recent sermons.

It is critical that you have a website for your initiative. In fact, you will probably need more than one. Name it something relevant, like YorkFestival.com, YorkFestival.org, and YorkFestival.net. The .net address might be used for communication to the team, while the .com or .org address would be your public website. You could also use what are called subdomains, such as "team.YorkFestival.org" for your private team website. Another use of the subdomain is as a subdivision of your efforts, such as youth.YorkFestival.org. Typically, for most hosting companies, the subdomains are free with your main domain. Most host packages also come with hundreds of e-mail addresses, so you could give all your team members an e-mail address that relates right back to the initiative. You might also want to make them functional e-mail addresses, such as Youth@YorkFestival.org.

Your website will be the anchor for all your promotional efforts. Your print advertising, radio, and video advertising will all refer back to the website for more information. It is your storefront, so to speak. When designing your website, use the same rules as those for a poster as presented previously. And have it done professionally. In fact, there is probably an excellent web designer right there in your city church who is just waiting to be asked. If possible, your website should utilize tools such as audio podcasts and YouTube video links right there on the main website page.

Your private website will be your means of communicating with the church and team. It should require a username and password for access. You might want to include a bulletin board on it so questions can easily be asked and answered. An alternative to consider is a Facebook.com site with restricted access. You will also want your initiative and IMPACT events posted on social networking sites such as Facebook and Twitter.

Radio

While for the younger crowd mp3 and iPod players have eclipsed radio, it is still a valid advertising medium, especially on the drive-home and drive-to-work times. Radio is also cheaper than nearly all other advertising mediums, so do not neglect this tool, especially as you draw closer to the time for the IMPACT events. Once you have created your radio ad, place it on your website as well.

Podcasts and YouTube Videos

These are audio and video files for Internet sharing, and they are especially critical for the youth culture. They are also relatively easy to create. The Apple App Store offers a free podcast assistant, and Final Cut Pro, a video-production application, is not very expensive. Most cellular phones today can make videos good enough for use on the web.

Television

Though you can inexpensively produce a pretty good video for the web, it is a different story for television. Television ads need to be done professionally, both in design and production. And they are expensive. But the payback, especially in large cities, is tremendous. Conversely, television has become extremely diverse, with over a hundred channels on the typical provider's lineup, so the question becomes where to put your ad. Always remember to stay customer focused and place your ad in the time slot most likely to grab your customers, which is probably during the evening news. For cities that are more remote and rely on broadcast stations many miles away, TV is probably not the best tool to use.

Inexpensive Alternatives

Word of Mouth and Direct Marketing

You will use this quite a bit, and we discuss it in more detail in the next chapter.

Press Releases

I previously mentioned my thatched-home business. One of our most successful advertising events was a free article in the newspaper. It was a full one-page spread on the front page of the business section, with color photos included, and it was available simply for the asking. My son just called the reporter, told him what we were doing, and set up a time for him to come out. The article appeared in the next Monday's business section, covering the entire front page—a totally free ad, professionally done, and right on the front page of the business section! This was the most effective advertising we ever did, though it wasn't technically advertising at all.

Whenever you have an event involving the public that you think might be newsworthy, such as a mini prayer fair, call the appropriate reporters from the newspaper and the television station. In most cases, they will want to come out and report it. At the very least, write a press release and submit it for publication.

A newspaper will generally have a certain format they want to use in their press releases. Your job is to follow their format, of course, but more importantly, you need to think like a journalist. Ask yourself what the reporter is going to look for. First of all, the information must be news; it cannot be old information. It also must be newsworthy; that is, something fresh and enticing. This is called "the hook," and it is important because that is what is going to attract a journalist and make him or her want to print your story or, even better, to attend the event and report on it directly. A typical format for a press release follows:

Date
FOR IMMEDIATE RELEASE
For more information, contact: (Provide your name, your phone number, your e-mail address.)
Headline (Use the hook.)
Body text (Put the bait on the hook.)

Here are some tips for your press release:

- Include something helpful that the reporter can quote, such as tips, rules, or principles.
- Keep it brief. Let the newspaper call for more information, but offer the courtesy of respecting their time.
- Send releases to every local editor in your area, no matter how small the publication.
- Do not make any errors, grammatical or information wise.

Church Signs

These are peppered all over your city. Don't overlook their use as mini billboards. They can be used as if they were those billboards, and they are totally free!

This media blitz is going to be incredibly expensive. For a city with a population of fifty thousand, the cost will run into hundreds of thousands of dollars. The cost for larger cities may actually be in the millions. I don't mean to scare you away from effective promotion; you just need to be prepared. When you think about it, a city of fifty thousand probably has fifty churches, so when you consider the church's mission and the expected outcome of a transformed city, each church's need to come up with a few thousand dollars should not be a huge inconvenience. There are also numerous businesses that recognize the importance of such an endeavor and would be willing to underwrite a portion of the advertising (it's a tax deduction for them). Recruit a good fund-raiser. There is probably already one in your city church that God has waiting for the opportunity. There are also numerous inexpensive or free options for promoting your events, so use those to the maximum, but do it well and do it professionally. Sloppy promotion is counterproductive.

To help reduce costs associated with promotion materials, Grace Promotion has developed material that can be used directly or customized for individual use. This material is available at a very reasonable cost. Simply navigate the web to Gracepromotion.org. to see what is offered.

Chapter 8

Into Battle: IMPACT Events

It's time for battle—not in the sense of hand-to-hand combat or even armed conflict, but in the sense of taking back lost ground. It's time to go after the unredeemed lost souls in the city. It's time for the harvest!

For this chapter, I am going to alter the picture a bit. Up until now, we have been viewing the city-transformation process as a battle between the saints of God and the spiritual forces of darkness. This is true, of course, but by this point in the process, the enemy has been so severely weakened that we can just go in and plunder the city, so to speak. So it is much more appropriate to look at this phase as a harvest. We have planted the seed, tended the crops, and now it is time to harvest.

To date, if you have been using this book as a guide, you have gathered together in unity both the spiritual leaders of your city and the church body located throughout your city. As a result, you have disarmed the spiritual forces of the enemy. You have set new angelic guards at the gates of the city and kicked out the demonic ones. Then you gathered with other like-minded believers and targeted prayers for each individual person in the city. All this has been going on for a while now, like the sun shining down on plants to ripen them for harvest. Finally, you fertilized and watered the crops by having a massive media campaign to awaken the people of your city to the idea of having a relationship with God Himself. At long last, the crops are now ripe, perhaps even overripe, and harvest time has arrived. So let's go bring it in!

Your IMPACT events must be radical and infused with fun for the whole family

This harvest is going to require special tools. The methods of the past are *not* going to make it anymore. In the first half of the last century, evangelists traveled the countryside and held meetings in large tents. It was considered normal for the populace to attend these events, and they were, to a large degree, effective. The practice of holding tent meetings changed in the second half of the century to using large auditoriums, but the format remained essentially the same, emphasizing singing and preaching.

In our current culture, this kind of event is no longer effective. Yes, the church today might attend such an event—well, at least part of the church. But the unchurched in today's culture would stay away. Events today, though maintaining the essential components of worship and preaching, must present something more in order to attract the unchurched. Creativity and prayer are required to develop powerful IMPACT events.

Your IMPACT events must be radical and infused with fun for the whole family if you hope to entice attendance. Perhaps you could consider a fair or festival setting with fun events and booths commingled with ministry booths. You could cap this off with a concert, worship, and preaching, followed by signs and wonders. This is just a suggestion and merely one example. The point is, your team needs to spend time in prayer to create events that go beyond those of the past. There is a reason those kinds of events are not typically done anymore—they don't work in today's culture! Even though your events will have a new cloak on them, the essentials of worship and preaching need to remain because they are biblical principles.

The youth events need to expand beyond even the radical nature of the main events. You will need to be relevant to youth in radical ways. I highly recommend that you look at Ron Luce's Acquire the Fire events and follow his example. He has been changing kids' lives for a couple of decades now, and he continually changes his techniques in order to fit the ever-changing youth culture.

Enough said about the events. Make them radical and meaningful. Maintain your customer focus. The actual evangelist selected is unimportant. Yes, you have to use someone with that particular ministry gift, but the fruit will be so ripe and the Holy Spirit's presence so strong that the actual preacher will be largely immaterial. You presently have that ministry gift present in your city church, so there is no need to bring in a high-power evangelist unless God particularly leads you in that direction.

Preparations for IMPACT

This chapter focuses on the couple of weeks prior to the IMPACT events and the events themselves. Over the past several months, the youth team has been busy planning their event, as have the children's team and the adults' team. The worship teams have been practicing. The logistics team has arranged for all the facilities and equipment necessary for the IMPACT events. The counselors are in the process of training for the harvest. The media team is very involved in its blitz. And you have just completed a citywide week-long fast.

Every member of the church has been praying for every citizen of your city. Now it is time to put feet to those prayers. A month or so ago, each family was contacted to see if they had any prayer needs, and you prayed with them as they requested it. Some people have already been won to the Lord as a result of your actions. Now it is time to go to each one of those families and personally invite them to the IMPACT event. When you invite them, actually offer to escort them there or give them a ride if they need it. Go out of your way to help them get there. You may encounter some resistance, but over the past several months, you have learned how to deal with that—you don't, but you pray and let God deal with it. Remember, the most powerful tool for breaking chains is fasting. If someone is adamant about not attending, pray and fast.

The IMPACT Events

With great anticipation, you have worked up to this climactic event. It has been hard work and continues to be. All the teams are now in active participation roles, ushering, leading worship, and bringing people to the events. The intercessors are still praying, and the counselors are still working. But oh, the satisfaction when you reach this point! I have organized and led events such as this, and there is just nothing like the culmination and fulfillment experienced during the altar call or the healing line that forms after the event. I remember once standing in the back of the facility as people streamed forward to answer God's call to receive Jesus and His redemption. Tears were streaming down my face as unspeakable joy swept over me. I had obeyed and allowed God to work through me, and this was the result. There is nothing like it. Nothing compares to this.

Though these events require a great deal of hard work, they actually flow all by themselves. It's the preparation, planning, and cleanup that are difficult. Challenges will always occur, but they are handled one at a time and solved. The events kind of take care of themselves. Keep on holding these events until people stop coming or the Holy Spirit says to stop. This could go on for a month or so.

Each of the new converts needs to leave with a packet of information and a Bible. The packet should include a booklet with information about all the churches represented in this endeavor. Also included should be information on the next steps the new converts should take.

Despite all the current success, the work is not yet complete. Let's move on to the next phase.

Chapter 9

Rebuilding: The Discipleship Phase

The battle is over. Victory is won. Small skirmishes remain, but for the most part, peace and safety rule the streets. Vast numbers have been rescued from the rule of the tyrant and translated into the Kingdom of God's dear Son. Churches in your city are bulging at the seams—so much so that you actually want church planters to come in and relieve some of the pressure. So what's next? Is it over, or is there still more to do?

Jesus' mandate as He was leaving this earth was to go and *make disciples* of all people. Evangelism was not His mandate, though that is part of it. Making disciples implies that we first must evangelize, but that is just the first step. Your job at this point is incomplete. Just bringing masses of people to salvation is only the beginning. A lot of work remains. Now we enter the discipleship phase.

I have been an engineer for much of my adult life, and we engineers know that the *law of entropy* prevails in our world: without outside influence, things left to themselves will degenerate or degrade over time. This is true in discipleship also; therefore, we need to take positive steps to disciple all new converts to prevent them from slipping back into their old ways.

Actually, in the beginning, many will still be living in accordance with their old ways because they know no other lifestyle. Still, the Holy Spirit has been at work. The bully discussed in chapter 1 stops bullying as the Holy Spirit prompts and convicts him in his spirit; the pregnant teen changes her mind about getting an abortion and now decides to keep her baby; the gang meetings turn into Bible studies even though the members have no idea what to study; and the gambler suddenly stops gambling. Much has changed as a result of the work of the Holy Spirit, but something more must be done to put these folks on a path to absolute victory and keep them from sliding back into their old lifestyles. City transformation cannot happen until actual changes in lifestyle by each person takes place. Discipleship training is the key to seeing this accomplished. There remains a lot of work to do, so let's get to it.

Good discipleship programs and curriculums abound, and there are a wide variety of tools to use. Some programs are structured as a classroom series offered one night a week for several weeks, while others are a compilation of several sermon series. Regardless of the specific program and tools used, two things must happen to effect the desired transformation in your city: (1) individual lifestyles must change to conform to a biblical lifestyle, and (2) consistent, homogenous biblical truths must be imparted. The church in your city needs to have a common biblical foundation. The individual denominational doctrines can remain (as long as they are biblical), but a common set of truths must be consistent throughout the city church to facilitate unity, harmony, love, and biblical lifestyles. This common set of truths held by the entire church, will effect your city transformation.

For several years, I had been troubled by the lack of true disciples in the church—those who actually walked the scriptural walk. I would read the Bible and see what it said but then would look at the church and see something different. I did not make this observation in a condemning way; it was more of an analytical query. What was the cause of the lack of true disciples?

My own personal spiritual growth had come from a variety of sources: Sunday sermons, tape messages from a variety of anointed teachers, books, seminars, and of course the Bible and Holy Spirit Himself. This growth came over several decades and was very disjointed. Basically, each time the Holy Spirit taught me something new, I had to readapt what I had learned previously. My learning was based on where I happened to be at the time and what the preacher/teacher happened to be teaching at the time—a very inefficient curriculum.

Pondering the church's lack of disciples, I realized my experience of spiritual growth was true of many other Christians as well. I was particularly sensitive to this condition because I have a master's degree in occupational training, focusing on apprenticeship training, so I knew what a good systematic training program was supposed to look like. I really hoped that someone would develop a discipleship-training curriculum to correct this problem. I probably even shot a few prayers up for God to find someone to do it.

Sometimes I wish that God would have answered my prayers in a different way, but He didn't. Perhaps, unknown to me, He placed it on someone else's heart to develop a discipleship program. That is entirely likely. However, I do know how He answered the prayer to me personally.

I was driving home from work one day in 2007. At the time, I had a one-hour commute each way. It was a normal day of commuting, and I had some Christian music playing softly as I drove down the highway. All of a sudden, completely out of nowhere and completely foreign to my thought process at the time, God invaded and told me to develop a discipleship curriculum. When God speaks to me in this fashion, things typically start exploding inside me. And they did this time as well. I could see in general the topics to be covered, and I could also see that it was to be developed using the curriculum-development concepts I was familiar with from the knowledge gained while pursuing my master's degree.

The curriculum would be systematic and produce Christians who were actually fruitful and capable of walking in the principles of Scripture on a daily, continual basis. The title of the curriculum was to be the Fruitful Disciple Series, based on John 15:8. Curriculum developers use a certain process to create a course of study, and already armed with that knowledge, I started in on the task. I added another dimension, though: prayer. I allowed the Holy Spirit to direct the process and change the content as He willed. The process started with the development and definition of the characteristics of a fruitful disciple, and I allowed the Holy Spirit to define those. From those characteristics flowed the individual modules of the series. I have been amazed at what has transpired as a result of this Spirit-led process.

God gave me the strategy for winning and transforming cities in the late nineties. I always knew that the missing discipleship part was a huge gaping hole in the strategy, and perhaps that is why I was so desperate for a good discipleship series. Since God had not given me that part, I assumed He would give it to someone else or provide it to each city that used the strategy. This new direction in 2007 to develop the Fruitful Disciple Series, however, provided the missing piece of the city-transformation strategy. To accomplish the city transformation you desire, it is not necessary to use this particular discipleship series. However, it *is* necessary to find something that builds a thorough, solid foundation and can be used throughout the city church.

The Fruitful Disciple Series is based on Scripture and Scripture alone. There was a concerted effort to avoid any denominational doctrines. Its purpose is solely to develop solid, fruitful followers of Jesus Christ. While it is not necessary that you use this specific curriculum, it is nonetheless a good model to follow as you research the curriculum your city should use. With that in mind, a synopsis of what the series includes is presented in the rest of this chapter as a guide for your own discipleship program.

The Fruitful Disciple Series

Overview and Purpose

The normal "Christian" life as we see it today is by and large just an added feature to the normal soulish, or secular, life. For many people, Christianity is just something they do in addition to the other things they do, like pursuing a hobby or avocation. The Bible, though, demands that we become new persons altogether, walking in accordance with the Spirit and not the world. We are to walk as Jesus walked. We are supposed to develop our newly born spirits so that they are in charge of our lives.

Some Christians attempt to blend a soulish Christian life with the spiritual one and can be somewhat effective, though still "of the world" to one degree or another. Very few are fruitful disciples living by the Spirit, and that is understandable because until now there has been no readily available tool to bring them to that level. Of course, the Bible and individual Bible studies, books, sermon tapes, preachers, and even college courses have always been accessible, but there has been no systematic training curriculum to renew the mind and put the disciple on the track of becoming a fruitful disciple, one who is in the world but not of it.

The Fruitful Disciple Series is a set of training engagements that offers the minimum amount of training necessary to be fruitful in the Christian life. By no means is this training series exhaustive on the subject of Christian living; it is meant merely as a starting point. The fifteen modules build on one another, so if you were to proceed through these in the order intended and applied the principles, upon completion you would have sufficient knowledge and skill to begin living a fruitful Christian life.

Module 1: Redemption—Purchased from Slavery

As we embark on this journey to becoming a fruitful Christian, it is important to first understand what a Christian is so that we can then make it fruitful. What exactly did Jesus purchase for us? If you say "salvation," you would be correct, but what is salvation? I really don't think this term is understood by those who are not Christians or fully by those who are. Most Christians understand that to be saved is to accept Jesus as Savior. Okay, what does that mean? When I have asked Christians this question, I have found that most cannot provide a good answer. This is even truer of nonbelievers.

The first module contains ten lessons to develop this foundational topic:

- Why Redemption Is Necessary
- What Redemption Is
- Redemptive Acts of Jesus I: Spirit Regeneration
- Redemptive Acts of Jesus II: Righteousness
- Redemptive Acts of Jesus III: Eternal Life
- Redemptive Acts of Jesus IV: Reinstatement of Rulership
- Redemptive Acts of Jesus V: Peace
- Redemptive Acts of Jesus VI: Healing
- Redemptive Acts of Jesus VII: Holy Spirit
- Lifestyle Outcome

Module 2: Covenant and Communion

One of the things we have to establish before we go any deeper into this Christian life is the concept of God's love for us. Unless we establish this, how can we ever believe He will do anything for us or for anyone we minister to? We saw in the previous module how we all are in need of redemption and all the things that are wrapped up in that redemption. But really, does the God of the universe actually care about little old me or you individually? Is that really true?

Abraham, the guy the Bible calls the "father of faith," had a hard time with that concept too. He knew that God was God and that he had to obey Him, but . . . when it came to God's desire to give him something, Abraham had a hard time with that. He just could not wrap his head around the concept that the big, super God of the universe wanted to give him something. God used the blood covenant to help Abraham understand just how much He loved him. Then Jesus became the mediator of the new covenant with new and better promises, and He wrapped that up in communion.

This module has only three lessons, but they are critical to understanding and comprehending the love that God has for us.

Module 3: Living in God's House—The Power of Abiding

The theme scripture for this entire Fruitful Disciple Series is John 15:8: "This is to my Father's glory, that you bear much fruit, showing yourselves to be my disciples." John 15 has much to say about living a fruitful Christian life, and of all the inspired writers of the Bible, John says the most about actually living the life. He is also the one who said we must walk as Jesus did. So John 15 is the reference text for this module.

This module is the most important module in the entire Fruitful Disciple Series. It is the key to an abundant Christian life. If the students get this and nothing else, they will have gained tremendously. All the other modules either define what a Christian is or provide guidance on some aspect of the Christian life. This is not to say that the other modules are not important to being a fruitful disciple, just that this one is the *key* to the *life* itself.

There are seven lessons in this module:

- What Is Abiding?
- Life in the Vine
- Apart from Me
- Living Words
- Love in the House
- Joy in the House
- Summary

Module 4: Kingdom Attitudes—Prince, Pauper, or Jester?

One might ask, "Why is there an entire module on the subject of a kingdom?" Well, the answer is that Jesus talked about it. In fact, that is pretty much *all* He talked about. In the Gospel of Matthew, the subject of the kingdom of heaven, or kingdom of God, is discussed over forty times. Matthew 4:23 says Jesus preached the "good news [or gospel] of the kingdom." For some reason, the church has shortened that to just the "gospel" and pretty much ignored the entire concept of the kingdom. But we need to learn about the kingdom because it is integral to life as a fruitful disciple.

The kingdom of God is discussed well over a hundred times in the New Testament, and we need to clearly understand what it means and then respond accordingly. In truth, this subject could become a course in and of itself because there is so much reference to it and depth in it, but we will only introduce the concept in this module in order to understand the attitudes associated with it.

There are ten lessons in this module, most focusing on a particular attitude that a fruitful disciple should develop:

- Seeking the Kingdom
- What Is a Kingdom?
- Reverence
- Respect
- Meekness
- Royalty
- Authority
- Humility
- Confidence
- Valor

Module 5: Prayer—So You Want to Talk to . . . God?

This module develops the overall subject of prayer, starting with the definitions and biblical mandates concerning prayer. There are also lessons on each of the basic types of prayer. Additionally, the module covers the subject of targeting prayers, prayers that get the job done.

The lessons in this module include the following:

- Types of Prayer
- Devotions
- Private Prayer
- Group Prayer
- Public Prayer
- Intercessory Prayer
- Binding and Loosing
- Confession
- Fasting
- In the Spirit
- Spiritual Warfare
- Throne-Room Prayers

Module 6: Fruit Started It; Fruit Ends It

The Fruit module is another attitudinal module, but it does not deal with mental attitudes. The fruit of the Spirit is just that—fruit *of the Spirit*. However, developing this fruit does require a renewing of the mind to allow the fruit to manifest.

There are ten lessons in this module:

- Introduction
- Love
- Joy
- Peace
- Patience
- Kindness
- Goodness
- Faithfulness
- Gentleness
- Self-Control

Module 7: Holy Goose Bumps! What's This Holy Spirit Stuff?

The subject of the Holy Spirit can be a controversial subject, so we just stick with the Bible and what it has to say about it. All that is required is that you keep an open mind as you go through these eight lessons:

- The Trinity
- The Holy Spirit Throughout the Bible
- The Holy Spirit and Jesus
- The Indwelling Holy Spirit
- Baptism in the Holy Spirit
- Gifts of the Holy Spirit
- Fruit of the Holy Spirit
- Modern-Day Examples

Module 8: Witnessing

This is a short module and mostly a practice session. Most Christians are just not comfortable witnessing, so this module dispels the fears associated with it and gives practical methods and advice for winning the unredeemed.

Module 9: Heroes

This module does not delve into the theology of the Old Testament, but rather it focuses on the characteristics that define the heroes of the Bible and how those characteristics can also be developed in the fruitful disciple. The Hall of Faith of the Bible describes some of their exploits in verses 33–35 of Hebrews 11:

> Who through faith conquered kingdoms, administered justice, and gained what was promised; who shut the mouths of lions, quenched the fury of the flames, and escaped the edge of the sword; whose weakness was turned to strength; and who became powerful in battle and routed foreign armies. Women received back their dead, raised to life again. There were others who were tortured, refusing to be released so that they might gain an even better resurrection.

A lesson is devoted to each of these seventeen heroes:

- Noah
- Abraham
- Joseph
- Moses
- Joshua
- Caleb
- Gideon
- Esther
- David
- Solomon

- Elijah
- Elisha
- Daniel
- Shadrach
- Peter
- Paul
- John

Module 10: Faith—Stepping Out

Since we now have a biblical foundation of how faith worked for the biblical heroes, we can learn how to develop it in our own Christian walk. We start by understanding what faith is and developing a definition for it. Then we learn how faith works and its relationship to other fruits of the Spirit like patience and love. We also learn what faith is not. Finally, we move into practical application with some exercises to do.

Module 11: Healing and Health

Jesus purchased our healing, but it seems that it is very hard for most of us to receive this as part of our redemption. In this module, we develop a solid biblical foundation for healing, and we look into the things that could hinder healing in our own bodies and in those to whom we minister. We also consider the ministry of healing and how to walk in that ministry.

Module 12: The Devil

Is there really a devil? How did he come about? Is he all-powerful, all-knowing? What's his past, future? Does he have helpers? Are demons real? What can they do to us? All these are questions discussed in the five lessons of this module.

Module 13: Ministries—What Am I Supposed to Do?

There are spiritual-gift ministries and things that just need to be done, things that God calls us to do and things that He just expects us to do. We discuss them all and try to enable the students to be specific about their own particular ministries.

Module 14: Finances—"They Always Talk About Money"

This module develops the overall subject of finances from a biblical perspective. Jesus discussed money more than any other single subject, so it must be important. This module examines some of those scriptures and includes the following lessons:

- Introduction
- Tithing
- Seedtime and Harvest
- God's Promises
- Debt
- Balancing Motivations
- Faith and Giving
- Firstfruits
- Budgeting, Faith, and the Use of the Principles

Module 15: Christian Living—Living the High Life

In this module, we cover those key attributes that characterize a fruitful disciple. Some of them we recap, while others are newly introduced here. The lessons include the following:

- Introduction
- Abiding
- Love
- Obedience
- Holiness

- Authority
- Bold Action
- Wisdom
- Family
- Balance

"Balance" is the last lesson in the Fruitful Disciple Series. Some students may feel that they have been overloaded with so much during this course. It is easy for them to latch on to only a part of what was presented and get out of balance. This lesson puts all that has been taught into proper perspective so that the new disciples can be fruitful and multiply.

The online version of the Fruitful Disciple Series is free. You may access the course at FruitfulDisciple.com. There is also a classroom version of the series, including instructor guides, tests, and learner modules, that may be purchased via the same website.

Chapter 10

A City Reborn: Maintaining Revival

The battle is over. Victory is won. Small skirmishes remain, but for the most part, peace and safety rule the streets. Vast numbers have been rescued from the rule of the tyrant, and he has been run out of town. It's time to celebrate!

Now is the time for dancing in the streets—God has done something marvelous for you—so gather the church in one huge celebration. Let it be an event designed to give God thanks and glory for what He has done. You have worked hard, but He has done it, and only He gets the glory.

Once that is done, the participatory board needs to gather once again. At this solemn event, the leaders of the city need to dedicate and consecrate this reborn city to God and affirm anew the covenant with Him to never again walk in disharmony. You have demonstrated the power of a united city-wide church. You must never again turn back to your old backbiting, unloving ways. Pledge this together.

Though most of the people in your city have discovered a new, vital relationship with Jesus, a few are taking their time about committing to this new relationship. Repeated smaller events and ongoing efforts need to be undertaken to bring these lost sheep into the fold.

There will be repeated attempts by the enemy to regain all the footholds he once had in your city. You absolutely and resolutely must stand against him, while acting in love toward all people. Do not become complacent, even in unity. You must continually claim your promise and walk in it. Don't let the enemy back into your city.

As I write this last chapter of this book, I am awestruck by what God has done in your community. You have gathered together in unity and claimed the promise of Psalm 133. You have taken up arms against the demonic forces ruling your city and soundly defeated them and expelled them from your midst. You have prayed for each and every nonbeliever in your community, and that prayer has spawned a new love for the people in your city. You have held events designed to bring the lost into a vital relationship with a loving God, and you are now discipling them.

God has done a great thing for you—something you could not have done for yourself—and I am awestruck by Him. He is so beautiful, so awesome, so loving. There is none like Him. To Him be the glory!

Freely you have received; now freely give. Become a sister city to another city and help it through this process. Help it with prayer, with logistics, and with finances. To solidify what God has given you, give it away.

CPSIA information can be obtained at www.ICGtesting.com
Printed in the USA
LVOW011420191211

260147LV00005B/18/P

9 781619 046078